# While Waiting

## The Waiting Journey

**Carla L. Chatman**

Scripture quotations marked (NIV) are taken from the Holy Bible, New International Version®, NIV®. Copyright © 1973, 1978, 1984, 2011 by Biblica, Inc.™ Used by permission of Zondervan. All rights reserved worldwide. www.zondervan.com The "NIV" and "New International Version" are trademarks registered in the United States Patent and Trademark Office by Biblica, Inc.™

Copyright © Carla Chatman 2025

ISBN: 9798274398763

No part of this publication may be reproduced, distributed, or transmitted in any form or by any means, including photocopying, recording, or other electronic or mechanical methods, without the prior written permission of the publisher, except in the case of brief quotations embodied in critical reviews and specific other noncommercial uses permitted by copyright law. All rights reserved.

For permission requests, write to
Carla Chatman
PO Box 820332
N. Richland Hills, TX 76182

# *Dedication*

*To the millions who find the challenge of waiting unbearable: may you stay in peace, grow in character, and discover how important you are to God.*

*Trust the process and keep it movin.'*

*To my grandson, Jason Bruton, and my goddaughter, Jayde Duncan: I believe you will reach your goals. Trust each process, know the work is worth it, and remember you are deeply loved and prayed for.*

*To my sons, Travis (with Kristi) and Zachary, and my granddaughter, Kyra: you are my joy and my why.*

*Every lesson I've written here, I carry because of you.*

# *Thank You...*

for purchasing this book. To support your journey beyond these pages, download the free **Waiting Journey Prayer & Declaration Guide**. It was created to walk alongside this book and help you stay grounded, focused, and hopeful while you wait.

Also, don't forget to leave a review on Amazon.

# Acknowledgments

No journey is walked alone.

To my family, thank you for standing beside me through seasons of waiting and reminding me that love never quits.

To my friends, mentors, and church community, thank you for your encouragement and prayers when silence felt heavy.

To my Big Brothers Big Sisters family and the young people I've mentored, you've inspired me more than you know. Your strength has fueled this book and my hope for the next generation.

# Table of Contents

A Note to the Reader ................................................. ix
Introduction: Why Waiting Feels So Hard................... xiii
PHASE I — GROUNDING ............................................. 1
   Chapter 1: The Struggle of Waiting ......................... 3
   Chapter 2: Purpose in the Pause ............................ 11
PHASE II – GROWING................................................. 19
   Chapter 3: Trusting God's Timing.......................... 21
   Chapter 4: Focus in the Wait ................................. 31
   Chapter 5: Rooted Faith in the Wait ...................... 39
PHASE III — GUARDING ............................................. 47
   Chapter 6: Prayer in the Wait ................................ 49
   Chapter 7: Guarding in the Wait ........................... 59
   Chapter 8: Warring in the Wait.............................. 67
PHASE IV-GLORIFYING ............................................... 75
   Chapter 9: Fasting in the Wait ............................... 77
   Chapter 10: Praise in the Wait ............................... 85
   Chapter 11: Mistakes and Setbacks in the Wait ....... 95
   Chapter 12: Thanksgiving as a Weapon................ 103
Chapter 13: Paying It Forward in the Wait ............... 113
Epilogue: The Gifts I Didn't Expect ......................... 121
Final Encouragement ............................................... 127
Appendix – Tools for the Waiting Journey ................ 131
Closing Blessing....................................................... 134

# A NOTE TO THE READER

This book is more than a one-time read; it's a companion for your journey. During your waiting season it's a place to pause, reflect, and remember that even in delay, purpose is being built.

Waiting doesn't move in straight lines. It loops, stretches, and circles back. Some days you'll feel progress; other days, you'll feel like you're standing still. Both matter. Both are part of your growth.

Each chapter includes stories, practices, and reflection prompts to help you notice what God is forming in you while you wait. You can read straight through, or skip to the section that fits your current season.

Most of all, come with an open mind. You don't need all the answers, just your questions, your hope, and your willingness to experience the journey as it unfolds.

My prayer is that these pages both encourage and equip you. May they remind you: waiting is not wasted. Every pause has purpose. And God is with you, even here.

# HOW TO USE THE REFLECTION PROMPTS

You'll find reflection and journal prompts at the end of each chapter. They aren't homework; they're invitations—to pause, to process, and to partner with God in your waiting.

Each chapter ends with a Reflection Pause — a short moment to stop, breathe, and take inventory of your heart. These aren't assignments; they're invitations.

Try these simple rhythms:

- Journal your responses. Write what comes first — don't overthink it.
- Talk them through. Share with a friend, small group, or mentor.
- Revisit them later. As your season shifts, your answers will too — and that's growth.

You don't have to finish them all at once. Let them stretch you gently. Some truths unfold slowly, and that's okay.

This is your space to slow down, listen, and see what's taking root beneath the wait.

## CIRCLE BACK WHEN YOU NEED TO

The journey isn't linear — every phase still has something to teach you.

**Weary?** Return to Grounding.

**Discouraged?** Spend time Guarding.

Just saw a **breakthrough?** Pause and Give thanks.

Each time you circle back, you'll notice something new — not because the book changed, but because you did.

## TIP FOR GROUPS

If you're reading with a friend, in a small group, or as part of a Bible study, use the prompts as discussion starters. Share as much or as little as you wish. And remember, your reflections may be the encouragement someone else needs.

**REMEMBER:** The goal isn't perfect words; it's connection with a perfect God. Every line you write is another way of saying, *"Lord, I trust You with my waiting."*

## Now that you've found your rhythm, let's begin the journey together.

While this book includes reflection prompts to help you pause and consider what God is doing in your waiting season, some journeys require more space to process, pray, and respond. The **While Waiting: The Waiting Journey Workbook** was created as a companion to this book for readers who desire a deeper, more intentional experience. The workbook provides guided journaling, extended prayer prompts, scripture meditation, and practical exercises that allow you to engage more fully with each phase of the journey. If you find yourself wanting to write more, reflect deeper, or walk this journey with greater clarity and focus, the workbook offers the structure and space to support you along the way.

# Introduction: Why Waiting Feels So Hard

## The Reality of Waiting

If you're holding this book, chances are you're in a season of waiting. Perhaps you are waiting for a promotion, a breakthrough, a relationship, healing, or clarity about your next step. Waiting comes in a hundred different forms, but the ache is always the same. It feels like time is moving for everyone else but standing still for you.

Waiting has a way of exposing things you'd rather keep buried. It strips away your sense of control. It forces you to sit with questions you can't answer. And if you're anything like me, waiting makes you restless, frustrated, and sometimes flat-out angry.

I didn't write this book because I figured waiting out. I wrote it because I've lived it, over and over again. Through military deadlines, adoption delays, career pivots, and personal storms, I've learned that waiting doesn't mean nothing is happening. It means something deeper is being formed beneath the surface.

## The Promise of This Journey

This book makes you a promise: your wait is not wasted.

The Waiting Journey will help you move from frustration to fulfillment through four distinct phases: *Grounding, Growing, Guarding, and Glorifying*. Each one shows you how to stand steady, grow stronger, and live with peace and purpose while you wait.

**The final sections, Giving and Going Forward, build upon these lessons, guiding you to share what you've gained and step boldly into what's next.**

You won't find quick fixes here. You'll find practices and stories that meet you where you are, in the tension between "not yet" and "almost." My hope is that you'll discover how every pause has purpose, and how waiting can be a sacred classroom, not just a holding pattern.

## Why This Book Exists

I authored this book because waiting nearly broke me, and because it built me.

There were seasons when I wanted to quit, cut corners, or stop believing altogether. But over time, I discovered something I didn't expect: waiting was shaping me. It was grounding my faith, clarifying my purpose, and teaching me to trust what I couldn't see.

This isn't a manual on how to wait faster. It's an invitation to see waiting differently, to notice that even when nothing seems to be moving, something holy is still happening.

## A Touch of Humor

Let's be real, waiting can make us do some ridiculous things. I've refreshed tracking numbers twenty times in one day, as if my obsession could make the package move faster. I've prayed for parking spaces as if God were managing logistics for my errands. I've told myself, *just five minutes on social media,* and an hour later, I'm comparing my life to a stranger's golden retriever that apparently travels more than I do.

Humor doesn't erase the ache, but it lightens it. Sometimes, the only way through waiting is to laugh at yourself and keep moving.

## Your Roadmap Through the Wait

Here's how the journey unfolds:

- **Part I – Grounding:** finding your footing when life feels unstable.
- **Part II – Growing:** practicing prayer, fasting, praise, and spiritual habits that stretch your strength.
- **Part III – Guarding:** learning to protect your heart, hope, and focus from discouragement or distraction.
- **Part IV – Glorifying:** giving thanks, paying it forward, and celebrating what God has done.

Each phase builds on the last, but you can start anywhere. The goal isn't perfection; it's presence.

## An Invitation

Waiting is hard. It always has been, and it always will be. But waiting can also be holy. It can be the place where God meets you most deeply, even in silence.

This book won't remove the ache of waiting, but it will help you walk through it with honesty, hope, and faith. Together, we'll navigate the slow seasons, the silent prayers, and the unseen work that happens beneath the surface.

Because your wait isn't wasted, it's working.

## An Invitation to Know Jesus

Before you turn the page, I want to remind you of something deeper than any waiting season: God's love for you.

If you've never begun a personal relationship with Jesus, this is your moment. Waiting can feel lonely, but you don't have to walk through it alone.

Jesus came so you could experience hope, forgiveness, and peace, right where you are, not after everything is fixed.

He knows every delay, every heartbreak, and every prayer you've whispered. And still, He loves you completely.

If you want to begin this relationship, you can do it right now with a simple prayer of faith:

> *"Jesus, I believe You are Lord and that God raised You from the dead. Forgive me for my sins and come into my heart. Teach me to walk with You and to trust You while I wait. Amen."*

If you prayed that prayer, welcome to the family of faith.

Your waiting now has a new companion, Jesus, who promises never to leave you and to walk with you through every season.

# PHASE I — GROUNDING

## FINDING YOUR FOOTING WHEN LIFE FEELS UNSTABLE.

# Chapter One

# The Struggle of Waiting

## When Waiting Feels Like Too Much

If you've ever been stuck waiting, you know it doesn't feel like growth. It feels more like standing in the world's longest line, watching everyone else breeze past while you shift your weight from foot to foot, clutching your ticket and wondering if they'll ever call your number. You start whispering questions under your breath: Why me? Why so long? Does this even matter?

Waiting can scramble your thoughts. You watch friends buy houses, toss wedding bouquets, post baby announcements, and launch businesses. Meanwhile, you keep refreshing your inbox, hoping for good news, or find yourself sitting, again, in a doctor's office, flipping through outdated magazines. It's like the universe handed out blessings and somehow skipped your name on the list.

That's when the questions start to swirl. Am I missing something? Did I let my chance slip away? Has God forgotten about me? Sometimes, the silence feels louder than any answer. For a long time, I thought silence meant abandonment. I had to learn, slowly and painfully, that silence isn't the same as absence.

The prophet once wrote, "The Lord is good to those whose hope is in him, to the one who seeks him; it is good to wait quietly for the salvation of the Lord" (Lamentations 3:25–26, NIV). Those words didn't erase my waiting, but they became a small light, a reminder that even in silence, there might be goodness I can't yet see.

## The Adoption Wait

My longest waiting season started in 1981; the day I placed my son for adoption. That wait didn't just last a handful of months or even a few years—it stretched on for nineteen. Nineteen years. Can you imagine that? That's nineteen birthdays with an empty seat at my table, candles never lit. It's graduations I missed. It's photo albums with blank spaces where his smile should have been, hugs that only happened in my imagination, memories that never had a chance to be made. Every year, the ache of absence grew a little sharper, echoing with all the "what ifs."

For a long time, it felt like those years were just slipping through my fingers, wasted and empty. Nothing about them looked holy or hopeful, they just hurt. But while I was aching, something was happening inside. When the reunion finally came, everything shifted. Looking back, I see those years hadn't vanished into thin air; they'd been quietly reshaping me. The waiting was forging a strength and tenderness in me, the kind my son would need from me when we finally met again. And even though I couldn't see it then, I know now those years were shaping him too.

Waiting became its own kind of classroom—silent, sometimes agonizing, but not without meaning. It didn't make the pain disappear, but it changed what the pain meant. What once sounded like silence started to hum with purpose. Looking back, it's clear: those years I thought were wasted were actually growing deep roots below the surface, preparing both of us for a moment that only God could orchestrate.

## The Garden Wait

While my adoption wait stretched on, life offered smaller, quieter lessons in patience. One spring, I decided to plant a flower garden. I watered faithfully, checked daily, and saw nothing. For weeks, the soil looked lifeless. I almost quit, convinced the seeds were dead.

But one morning, a tiny bud broke through the dirt. Life had been working beneath the surface all along.

That garden became a picture of my waiting season. Just because I couldn't see progress didn't mean nothing was happening. Growth often hides before it reveals itself. And here's the thing: waiting, as I learned, is never empty. It's where unseen roots take hold and quiet miracles begin.

## My Story with Waiting

My life has been one long lesson in waiting. Some waits were short and frustrating, like long lines at the DMV or sitting on a runway in the military for hours with no explanation. Others were devastating, like watching Hurricane Andrew flatten everything I owned or spending nineteen years waiting to be reunited with my son after adoption. Looking back, I can see how every kind of wait, big or small, wrote its own lesson into my story.

In the Air Force, I learned the strange rhythm of motion and stillness. Orders would shift, schedules would change, and we'd be ready to move, gear checked, uniforms sharp, adrenaline high, only to find ourselves grounded again. It was an odd kind of discipline, learning to stay ready while nothing happened. I carried that rhythm into life after service, and it felt the same. You prepare, you hustle, you pray, and then nothing. Silence. Delay.

But the hardest waiting I've ever endured was for my son. Nearly two decades of praying, crying, and longing. Holidays passed like mile markers. I carried hope like a fragile glass jar, trying not to drop it. There were seasons when I thought the wait had broken me. But when the reunion finally came, I realized the waiting had been shaping me all along.

## Everyday Struggles

But not all waiting happens in dramatic life stories. Sometimes it's small, everyday stuff. What I noticed is that these little moments can stack up, teaching us just as much as the big one, if we're paying attention.

Like sitting in traffic that makes you late, no matter how early you leave. Or waiting for test results, refreshing the patient portal like it might magically update. Or hitting "track package" six times a day as if FedEx might move faster because you're watching.

I've stood in grocery lines that moved slower than a snail on vacation. I've stared at my phone screen while it buffered in the middle of a show's best moment, yelling at Wi-Fi like it could hear me. I've sat in job interviews and then waited weeks for a callback that never came.

Those waits may seem small, but they wear on you. They test your patience in ways that stack up. And if you don't pay attention, the little delays can drain you just as much as the big ones.

## What Waiting Really Does

Here's the thing: waiting changes you, whether you like it or not.

It exposes what you rely on: comfort, control, validation. It shows you the cracks in your character, the shortcuts you want to take, the lies you're tempted to believe, the despair you have to wrestle. It also builds what nothing else can: patience, endurance, compassion, resilience.

But, I don't want to lecture you. I'd rather talk with you, as if we're sitting across the table with coffee or tea in hand. I get it. I know the sting of silence and the frustration of feeling stuck.

Your wait could look different than mine, maybe it's a scholarship, a child to be delivered from an addiction, a marriage restored, a new house, but the ache is familiar. Waiting has a way of making us feel powerless. But hidden underneath, something else is happening.

Roots are forming. Muscles are strengthening. Endurance is being built, even if all you see right now is delay.

## Humor in the Wait

Sometimes the only way to survive waiting is to laugh at yourself.

I've walked into the doctor's office ready to wait with grace, only to lose it when the clock ticked past my appointment time... twice. I had promised myself not to check an email again until the next day, but I checked it fifteen times before lunch. I once convinced myself I'd wait calmly for cookies to bake, but ended up opening the oven door every three minutes until they were flat and sad.

Waiting has a sense of humor. And sometimes, laughing at the absurdity is the only thing that keeps you sane.

## Closing

Waiting is messy, uncomfortable, and rarely neat. It may not look like progress, but something is growing underneath the surface. And one day, you'll look back and realize the wait wasn't breaking you, it was building you.

This is just the beginning of the waiting journey. Once you realize the struggle is real, the next step is learning that there's a purpose tucked inside the pause. That's where we head in Chapter Two: Purpose in the Pause.

## CHAPTER ONE NOTES

**Reflection Pause:** When waiting feels unbearable, what emotions rise to the surface first: fear, anger, doubt, exhaustion? Write them down honestly.

## CHAPTER TWO

# Purpose in the Pause

## When the Pause Feels Pointless

Have you ever felt like you're living in a freeze-frame; everyone else moving forward, while you're stuck on pause? That moment when you keep praying, showing up, believing, but it feels like nothing moves and life forgot to hit "play" again? That's the ache of the pause, and it's one of the hardest parts of any waiting season.

I've sat through pauses that felt cruel. I begged God for anything, a sign, a whisper, even a flicker of progress, and got nothing but silence. And silence doesn't just feel empty; it feels like rejection. It felt like my prayers got lost somewhere between earth and heaven. For a long time, I assumed that when God was quiet, He was absent. But what I've learned is that silence can be the sound of God still working, just not in ways I can see yet.

## Protection in Disguise

There's something sacred about pauses, though they rarely feel that way in the moment. They hold tension and purpose side-by-side. When you're caught between what was and what's next, it's easy to confuse stillness for punishment. But more often, it's protection, God slowing you down, so you don't wreck what He's still building.

I learned that in the Air Force. The rhythm was always "hurry up and wait." You'd prepare for days, lesson plans ready, emails sent, schedules lined up, and then? Nothing. No callback, no green light, just long stretches of "stand by." I used to think it was a waste of time. Later, I realized it was a practice in patience, learning to hold steady when the mission wasn't yet clear. Those pauses taught me that readiness isn't just about movement, it's about mindset. You must stay alert even when nothing's happening.

## The Inward Mirror

That lesson echoed years later in a wait that ran deeper and cut sharper than I ever imagined. When I placed my son for adoption, I never pictured the reunion taking nineteen years. Nineteen years of silence. Nineteen birthdays have passed without a phone call. Nineteen Christmas mornings with unwrapped gifts left under the tree and a quiet ache in the background. I spent nights lying awake, questions swirling in the dark: Was he safe? Was he happy? Did he know, somehow, that I loved him? Some days, the weight of those questions hollowed out any hope I tried to hold onto. I just wanted to skip ahead—to fast-forward through the uncertainty and land in the part of the story where everything made sense. But the pause seemed endless, heavier with every year that passed.

Now, looking back, I see it through new eyes. Those years weren't just gaps in my story; they were shaping me, line by line. The pause was quietly working in me, doing what only time can do: stitching up wounds, growing roots, building a foundation I didn't know I'd need. What I didn't realize then was that real faith isn't built on instant answers; it's grown in the hidden places, where nobody else can see. What I thought was a delay was construction.

The prophet Habakkuk said, "For the revelation awaits an appointed time; it speaks of the end and will not prove false. Though it linger, wait for it; it will certainly come and will not delay" (Habakkuk 2:3, NIV). That verse became my quiet anthem, though it lingers, wait for it. It whispered that God's timeline doesn't stall; it ripens. Waiting isn't empty space; it's just that the moment hasn't arrived yet.

## Hurricane Lessons

I've seen that same truth play out in both literal and spiritual storms. During Hurricane Andrew, I learned there are some seasons you can't rush. The night the winds roared through, all I could do was hunker down and listen to the house groan. Power gone, windows boarded, I sat in the dark with nothing but flashlights and faith. Hours passed like days. But looking back, I can see those hours were doing something in me. When the storm finally calmed, I stepped outside to find trees bent almost flat but not broken. Their roots had held. The pause in that storm hadn't looked like strength, but that's exactly what it was: endurance being born underground.

That's what God does in the pauses. He's strengthening what can't be seen. You think nothing's happening, but roots are gripping deeper. And later, when the wind comes again, and it always does, you'll realize the pause wasn't stillness after all; it was training.

## Everyday Pauses

Sometimes the pauses that shape us most aren't born of disaster but of the everyday.

- It's the traffic light that stays red just long enough to make you notice the sunset you would've missed.
- It's the spinning circle on your screen reminding you that not everything runs on your schedule.
- It's the hum of the waiting room, the chatter in the coffee line, the quiet minutes that slow you enough to breathe.

Those moments don't feel spiritual, but they expose something deeper, our craving for control.

We want God's promises on demand, not on delay.

But if you can learn patience in the small pauses, you'll have the endurance for the big ones. These everyday waits were preparing me for the bigger storms ahead.

Not every pause happens in isolation. Some unfold right in front of us, in carpool lines, coffee shops, or bleachers on a Saturday morning.

I've sat at youth games, watching parents shift restlessly on metal benches as the score stayed tied and the clock dragged. Nobody could speed it up. You just had to sit in it.

I've stood in coffee-shop lines where conversation turned strangers into neighbors, realizing that waiting sometimes creates space for connection we'd otherwise rush past.

## The Ache Meets the Pause

I've tried to rush both kinds of pauses, the everyday and the eternal, and it never works. Once, during a job review I thought would open a door, weeks turned into months of silence. I replayed every possible reason in my head. When the call finally came, the position I thought I'd missed turned out to be a mismatch all along. The offer I received later was a perfect fit for me. What I thought was denial had been protection. The pause had spared me from stepping into something that wasn't mine.

It's easy to measure progress by motion. But God measures it by maturity. The pause is His classroom, not His punishment. It's where He refines your focus, strips away distractions, and reminds you that purpose is rarely built at full speed. When life slows down, it isn't always a setback; it might be an invitation to see what you've been too busy to notice.

That's what happened in the long silence of my adoption wait. Somewhere between unanswered prayers and passing years, I stopped performing for God's approval and began sitting in His presence. I realized He wasn't asking for polished prayers; He was asking for honesty. He wasn't grading my faith; He was growing it. The pause became sacred, not because it was easy, but because it was real.

And then, one ordinary day, the pause ended. The reunion I'd prayed for nearly two decades finally arrived. My hands shook as I reached for my son, the one I'd carried first in my body and then in my prayers. That moment was holy. But so was everything that led up to it, the years of wrestling, doubting, surrendering. I used to think the wait was wasted time. Now I know it was the making of me.

## Closing

The truth is that pauses don't make sense while you're living them. They feel unfair, even cruel. But underneath the silence, something's always happening. Protection. Preparation. Quiet root work. Strength you don't realize you're building. One day, the stillness that once frustrated you will make sense; it was the forge where your future was formed.

Waiting reveals your struggle. The pause reveals your purpose. And both lead to something greater, timing. God's timing. That's where the next part of this journey takes us.

## CHAPTER TWO NOTES

**Reflection Pause:** What part of your life feels "on hold" right now? Instead of asking, *"Why is nothing happening?,"* try asking, *"What is God shaping in me while I wait?"*

# Phase II – Growing

**GROWTH HAPPENS QUIETLY IN THE SOIL OF FAITH, THROUGH TIMING, FOCUS, AND DEEPER ROOTS.**

# Chapter Three
# Trusting God's Timing

## When Time Feels Like the Enemy

One of the hardest parts of waiting is that the clock never seems to cooperate. Minutes crawl, weeks blur together, and years stretch so long you start to wonder if maybe God forgot you altogether. I can't tell you how many nights I sat staring at a calendar, convinced the clock was mocking me. Time felt like an enemy, instead of a gift.

I think back to seasons when I begged God to move faster, to make a decision, to bring about a breakthrough, or to fulfill a dream that felt stuck in limbo. Every delay cut deeper because I thought timing was everything. I thought I needed things to happen now. What I didn't understand was that waiting seasons weren't wasted time; they were shaping time. They were training me to see that God's timing isn't late, it's layered, woven with preparation I couldn't see yet.

## The Adoption Timeline

Nineteen years. That's how long I waited to be reunited with my son. At first, I thought it would be a year, maybe two. Surely not more than five. But one year bled into the next, and birthdays passed like shadows. Each one carried two emotions I couldn't separate: gratitude that he existed and grief that I wasn't there to see him grow.

There were moments I wanted to scream, "Enough already! God, haven't I waited long enough?" I wanted to fast-forward to the reunion, skip the silence, erase the pain. But here's the crazy thing: when the reunion finally came, I realized the wait itself had been doing something in both of us.

I wasn't the same woman who started the journey. I was stronger, steadier, and more prepared to be the mother he needed at that stage in his life. And he wasn't the same boy I had left. He had been shaped by his own story. We weren't meeting as strangers; we were meeting as two people who had been quietly molded during those nineteen years.

If the reunion had come earlier, it wouldn't have carried the same depth. The timing wasn't what I wanted, but it was what we needed. That's the maddening beauty of God's timing; you don't see the alignment until you're standing in it.

Paul put it this way: "If we hope for what we do not yet have, we wait for it patiently" (Romans 8:25, NIV). Waiting isn't wasted; it's evidence that hope is still alive, even when we can't see what's coming.

## Seeds and Soil

I learned long ago that tending that little garden, that growth begins underground. God's timing works the same way. You can't rush what's forming beneath the surface.

The roots stretch deep before anything green ever breaks through.

Waiting on God's timing feels a lot like that. You do the planting, you do the watering, and then you wait, often longer than you want. It feels like nothing is happening, but in reality, God is anchoring strength in unseen places before He allows what's been planted to rise.

That's the frustrating part of timing: the hidden work. We want quick results, visible progress, and proof that our effort matters. But God often works underground before He shows anything above ground. If He rushed the process, the roots wouldn't be strong enough to hold the growth.

## The Rhythm of Seasons

Time has its own language, and nature speaks it fluently.

I've stood outside and watched the sky shift from gold to gray as a day surrendered to night. You can't hurry a sunset; it unfolds at its own pace. The same with autumn leaves; they don't all change at once, they turn when they're ready. Even the ground rests between harvests, quiet but alive beneath the surface.

Those rhythms remind me that God's timing is never random. The slow fade of daylight, the steady return of spring, all of it whispers the same truth: growth takes time, and beauty doesn't rush to arrive.

Just like the earth moves through seasons we can't control, our lives do too. Some seasons look like bloom, others like bare branches. But every one of them matters, and each has its own appointed time.

What feels like a delay is actually protection. What feels like wasted time is actually preparation. Just like a seed knows when to break through, God's timing brings things to life exactly when they're ready, never too soon, never too late.

Wait for the Lord; be strong and take heart and wait for the Lord" (Psalm 27:14, NIV). Strength in waiting doesn't come from moving faster; it comes from holding steady when everything in you wants to quit.

## Everyday Timing Battles

You don't need a nineteen-year adoption journey or military experience to feel the weight of timing. It shows up in everyday life. Like leaving early for work only to hit every red light. Or sitting at the airport through delay after delay, wondering if you'll ever take off. Or watching your child reach milestones slower than others and learning that each one blooms on their own timetable. Timing confronts us in ways big and small, and it rarely bends to our schedule.

I remember standing in a line one day, frustrated that the cashier was moving more slowly than I thought possible. I was tapping my foot, huffing, already rehearsing my irritation in my head. Then I noticed the older woman ahead of me chatting with the cashier, her face lighting up because someone was actually listening to her.

That's the thing about timing: it humbles you. Whether you're sitting behind orange cones in a construction zone or waiting on a life-changing promise, it reminds you that God's pace doesn't bend to ours. Sometimes, the delay isn't about what He's doing for you, it's about what He's rebuilding somewhere else.

## Humor in the Wait

And let's be honest, timing loves a good punchline. I've asked God to hurry up, only to have Him answer in ways that felt straight out of a sitcom. Like the time I finally got the house I'd been praying for, and within days, the fridge sputtered and died, leaving me eating cereal with warm milk and laughing at the irony. Or the year I poured my hopes into a vision board, covering it with magazine dreams and prayers over every picture, then realized I hadn't included a single idea about how to pay for any of it.

Sometimes, the only thing to do is laugh at how upside-down it all seems. You just have to shake your head, grin at the chaos, and whisper, "Alright, God, I see Your sense of humor."

## Biblical Anchors for Timing

Story after story in Scripture reminds us that waiting is woven into the human experience. David was anointed as king while still a boy, but he spent years waiting in obscurity, running from Saul, hiding in caves, and shouldering responsibilities that looked nothing like royalty. Abraham and Sarah waited decades for the promise of a child. The Israelites wandered in the desert for forty years. Even Jesus lived thirty quiet years before stepping into public ministry.

None of those seasons was meaningless. David's hidden years weren't the end of the story; they were the setup for what God had already written. Abraham's long wait revealed his doubts but also refined his faith. The Israelites learned to depend on God in the wilderness. And Jesus' hidden years shaped Him for the work ahead.

God's timing rarely matches our clocks, but His pauses are never empty. They're loaded with purpose, even when all we see is delay.

## What Trusting Timing Produces

So, what comes out of all this waiting and trusting? For me, it's changed the way I see everything. The longer I wait, the more I realize just how narrow my own sense of timing is compared to God's wide horizon. Waiting has a way of shrinking my ego. I can make all the plans in the world, but I can't script the outcome. It's taught me endurance, too. After you survive one season of delay, you realize you can make it through the next. And trust? Waiting for what you want, and not getting it on your timeline, builds a different kind of trust, the kind that quietly says, "Even if this never goes my way, I still believe God's timing is good."

I've seen this same kind of fruit show up in other people's lives, too. I think of a young entrepreneur I knew, who spent years watching her business crawl along. She told me once, "If things had taken off right away, I would have lost everything. I wasn't ready yet." Turns out, timing wasn't out to get her. It was teaching her, shaping her, building her from the inside out.

## My Breakthrough in Trusting Timing

One of my breakthroughs came when I stopped treating time like a threat. Instead of asking, "Why not now?" I started asking, "What is God forming in me while I wait?" That shift changed everything. Suddenly, waiting wasn't punishment; it was preparation.

During the adoption wait, that perspective saved me more than once. During deployments, it steadied me. In everyday frustrations, it still reminds me that maybe, just maybe, there's something happening under the surface that I can't see yet. Trusting timing didn't erase the ache, but it gave me a way to stand in it without being crushed.

## Closing

When time feels like your enemy, remember; it's also your teacher. You may never love waiting, but you can learn to trust what's happening beneath the surface. Every delay is shaping you for something good you can't yet imagine. Take the next step with quiet courage; your story is still unfolding, and God is right on time.

This chapter is all about learning to trust God's timing. But trusting isn't passive; it requires focus. That's where we're headed next. Chapter Four takes us into the challenge of focusing in the wait, because once you've surrendered timing, the question becomes: where will you fix your attention?

## CHAPTER THREE NOTES

**Reflection Pause:** Think about your own season of waiting. Where have you felt most impatient with timing?

_____
_____
_____
_____
_____
_____
_____
_____
_____
_____
_____
_____
_____
_____
_____
_____
_____
_____
_____
_____
_____
_____

## Chapter Four

# Focus in the Wait

## When Focus Slips

Waiting has a way of scattering your attention. You start steadily, eyes on the goal, heart set on the promise, but the longer the silence stretches, the harder it is to stay centered. Distractions sneak in, doubts take over, and before long, you're staring at everyone else's lane instead of your own.

Psalm 37:7 (NIV) puts it plainly: *"Be still before the Lord and wait patiently for him; do not fret when people succeed in their ways."* That's the challenge, isn't it? Not just waiting, but waiting without measuring your pace against someone else's.

I've been there. In the military, orders changed so often that it was easy to drift into frustration instead of staying sharp. Later, in civilian life, the same thing happened: I checked my phone instead of working on what mattered, filling the day with noise because silence felt unbearable. Waiting can cloud your vision, making it easy to lose sight of your goals.

Focus isn't about gritting your teeth through stillness. It's about deciding, repeatedly, where you'll let your attention land. Because if you don't guide it, distractions will gladly take over.

## The Distraction Trap

Let me confess: I've lost focus in some truly ridiculous ways. I've wandered into rooms, stood there blinking, and had absolutely no idea why I came. I've sat down to "just check my email," only to look up twenty minutes later, somehow watching squirrels leap through backyard obstacle courses on YouTube. I've glanced at my vision board for a single minute, only to find myself scrolling through someone else's highlight reel and wondering when I fell off track.

But distractions aren't always the harmless kind that make you laugh. Sometimes, they slip in quietly and start to sting. They whisper, "You're falling behind," or "You'll never catch up." Before you know it, your gaze is glued to everything you lack, instead of what you're still holding onto.

A friend of mine, waiting for a kidney transplant, described her world to me. "Every time the phone rings, my heart skips," she said. She'd try to focus on her work or spend time with friends, but her thoughts always circled back to the same question: What if this is the call? Even sleep wasn't a refuge; her mind paced the floor all night. The waiting wasn't just slowing her down; it was sapping her strength. Distraction had taken the wheel.

That's why focus matters. It's not about pretending waiting doesn't exist. It's about making sure the wait doesn't swallow you whole.

## Everyday Battles for Focus

Focus gets tested in the smallest ways. For me, it looks like staring at a blank page when I'm supposed to be writing, then suddenly deciding the spice cabinet *must* be reorganized right now. Or committing to pray, only to remember halfway through that the laundry buzzer went off.

I've seen it in friends, too. A young mom waiting for her husband to come home from deployment told me she nearly lost herself in endless scrolling. "It numbed me," she admitted, "but it didn't help me." Eventually, she realized she needed new anchors: walking outside, journaling, and praying, not because these activities solved the wait, but because they kept her focus from slipping into despair.

Another friend, waiting for parole, said he battled distraction daily. "You can waste your mind in here if you're not careful," he told me. He chose to study, read, and even mentor younger inmates instead of letting his thoughts spiral out of control. He didn't have freedom yet, but he was training his focus, so he'd be ready when the door finally opened.

## My Military Training in Focus

Military life demanded focus like nothing else. Missions could shift in an instant, and chaos was always close by. We were trained to zero in, block out distractions, and stay alert, no matter how long the wait. That discipline carried over into waiting seasons outside the military.

Waiting feels like sitting through a long briefing where updates crawl in slowly. Every part of you wants to drift or check out, but discipline keeps your mind sharp and your spirit steady. Focus isn't about motion; it's about attention.

Sometimes, when my mind feels cluttered, I step outside for a minute. The Texas sun presses down, and a breeze pushes against my thoughts. Even the hum of passing traffic reminds me that movement is still happening all around me, even when my own season feels paused. That little reminder resets my focus: I can't control the pace, but I can stay present in it.

## Biblical Anchors for Focus

Scripture is full of scenes that point us back to where our eyes should land. Take Peter, stepping out of the boat, he's walking on water, heart pounding, until his gaze flickers to the churning wind and waves. At that moment, he starts to sink. It wasn't his feet that failed him, but his focus. Paul paints a picture of runners on the track, urging us to keep our eyes on the finish line instead of the competition. And the writer of Hebrews leans in with encouragement: fix your eyes on Jesus, especially when every part of you wants to give up, when the wait stretches on and on.

These aren't just words for people in the bible; they're real-life advice for the rest of us trying to hang on. They remind us of something we already feel deep down: wherever you set your focus, that's where your strength will follow.

## Humor in Losing Focus

Sometimes, losing focus while you're waiting is genuinely funny, at least once you're looking back on it. I've knelt in prayer, asking God for direction, and somehow ended up twenty minutes later elbow-deep in a bag of potato chips, alphabetizing my sock drawer as if my future depended on it. I once promised myself a TV fast to seek clarity, only to realize I'd memorized half the jingles from commercials playing in the background.

A friend once admitted her prayer journal was a mash-up of half-finished prayers and grocery lists. Another told me she'd just thanked God for "peace in the wait," only to completely lose her cool when her kids started arguing in the next room.

Waiting has this sneaky way of exposing just how human we are. But laughter is what keeps us afloat. Humor doesn't erase the struggle; it just makes sure we don't sink under the weight of it.

## What Focus Produces

Staying focused while waiting doesn't mean you never drift. It means you learn how to bring yourself back when you do. And over time, that practice produces something powerful.

**Focus produces clarity**. When you strip away distractions, you can finally see what matters.

**Focus produces peace**. When your attention is anchored, you stop being tossed around by every delay.

**Focus produces perseverance**. It trains you to stay steady, one day at a time, until the breakthrough comes.

**Focus produces freedom**, the kind that comes when you stop being ruled by everything you can't control and start choosing what you *can*.

## My Breakthroughs in Focus

One of my breakthroughs came when I realized that focus isn't about willpower, but rather about direction. I couldn't control how long my adoption wait lasted, but I could choose what I gave my attention to during those years. When I focused on bitterness, I sank. When I focused on gratitude, even small gratitude, I stood a little taller.

Another breakthrough came in a tight season when every dollar felt like a decision. I had every reason to spiral, bills stacking up, no relief in sight. But I forced myself to focus on small wins: the lights still on, laughter with friends, prayers that reminded me I wasn't alone. It didn't erase the weight of waiting, but it shifted me from despair to endurance.

## Closing

If your focus slips in the wait, you're not alone. The real strength is in choosing to return, again and again, no matter how distracted you feel. Each time you refocus, you're building the kind of endurance that will carry you through. Let every small return to clarity be a victory.

Focus steadies you in waiting, but endurance doesn't stop there. Faith takes root when focus deepens. That's where we head in Chapter Five: Rooted Faith in the Wait.

# CHAPTER FOUR NOTES

**Reflection Pause:** Where do distractions pull you hardest, comparison, anxiety, busyness, or numbing habits?

# Chapter Five
# Rooted Faith in the Wait

## Why Faith Feels Fragile in Waiting

Faith is easy to talk about when life moves smoothly. It's a different story when the time seems to crawl, prayers remain unanswered, and your surroundings don't reflect what you are hoping for. In waiting seasons, faith doesn't feel steady; it feels fragile.

I've had nights when my belief felt paper-thin, when doubt shouted louder than any sermon I'd ever heard. I've whispered prayers that sounded hollow even to me. And I've wondered if maybe I wasn't cut out for this whole "faith" thing at all.

But waiting has taught me something important: faith isn't about pretending you're unshakable; it's about planting yourself deep enough that when the storm hits, you may bend, but you don't break.

## The Adoption Wait and Faith's Roots

During my nineteen-year adoption journey, my faith was tested in ways I never expected. Every holiday without my son felt like another blow. Every unanswered prayer made me wonder if God had muted my line. There were nights I lay awake asking: *Do You see me? Do You care?*

What I didn't realize was that those questions weren't signs of weak faith; they were evidence of faith being stretched and strengthened. A tree doesn't grow roots in calm weather; it grows them when the wind shakes it. My belief was rooted not in outcomes but in God's character.

Looking back, I see that every tear, every frustrated prayer, and every time I chose to cling instead of quit all pushed my roots deeper.

## Everyday Roots of Faith

Faith in waiting isn't usually forged in big, cinematic moments. It's shaped in small, ordinary choices.

I think about a teacher who prayed for a promotion that never seemed to come. Instead of quitting, she poured her energy into her students every day, believing that her work mattered even if no one noticed.

Or a neighbor who longed for healing from chronic pain. She didn't always feel strong, but she chose to smile at people in the grocery store, to send notes of encouragement, to live as if her life was more than her diagnosis.

These weren't spotlight stories. They were quiet acts of perseverance that grew deep roots. That's where real faith lives, beneath the surface, in the hidden choices that no one sees but God.

## The Sports and Training Wait

Sports taught me the same lesson in a different language. Practices could feel endless, running drills, repeating plays, conditioning until my legs burned. Half the time, it felt like busywork that led nowhere, like we were training for training's sake.

But when game day came, I understood. The drills built muscle memory. The conditioning built stamina. The repetition built trust between teammates. What felt like wasted hours in the gym became the foundation that carried us when the pressure was on.

Waiting with God works the same way. It may look like nothing is happening, but those hidden reps are building something: strength, endurance, resilience. What feels like a delay is often preparation for the moment you'll need everything you've practiced.

## Biblical Anchors for Rooted Faith

Right in the pages of Scripture we see vivid portraits of what rooted faith looks like. Take Job, who lost nearly everything yet somehow found trust as his world collapsed around him.

Or Daniel, who stayed faithful even when obedience carried the risk of a lion's den; his consistency was born from a conviction that went beyond comfort.

Think about Ruth walking into an unknown future, choosing loyalty and hope over fear.

Noah kept building decade after decade before a single drop of rain fell.

Even the smallest acts of faith, like planting a mustard seed, can grow into something strong enough to shelter others. Story after story invites us to see that the waiting presses us toward deep roots; often starting small, but growing strong enough to last through storms.

## Humor in Faith Struggles

Faith in waiting can be raw, but it can also be funny. I've prayed for patience and lost it five minutes later in traffic. I've declared, "I'm standing on faith!"—then opened a new tab to Google backup plans. I've prayed bold prayers and immediately second-guessed them, like a kid ordering off a menu and wondering if they should've picked the chicken nuggets instead.

A friend once laughed about praying for God to guide her dating life while simultaneously swiping left and right on her phone. Another said she prayed for strength as a teacher, then thanked God when the fire alarm went off, giving her an unscheduled break.

Faith isn't always polished. Sometimes it's awkward, inconsistent, and hilariously human, and God's okay with that. He honors persistence more than perfection.

## What Rooted Faith Produces

Rooted faith doesn't make the waiting easy, but it does make you stronger. It's like working muscles you didn't know you had. Over time, you find endurance you never expected, the ability to keep going even when nothing seems to budge. It brings peace that doesn't add up on paper but somehow keeps your heart steady. And it offers a new way to look at things, reminding you that even when progress is invisible, growth is still happening somewhere beneath the surface.

Faith is what builds resilience. Every time you decide to trust again after disappointment, your roots dig a little deeper. Every time you whisper a shaky prayer instead of giving up, those roots spread a little wider.

Isaiah painted it like this: "Those who hope in the Lord will renew their strength. They will soar on wings like eagles; they will run and not grow weary" (Isaiah 40:31, NIV).

Roots do their best work underground, where nobody sees. Strength is forming, even when it all looks still. Renewal is happening in quiet places, in ways that matter most. Waiting might look idle, but beneath the surface, it's never wasted; it's where real work gets done.

## My Breakthroughs in Rooted Faith

One breakthrough came when I finally stopped mixing up faith with feelings. For the longest time, I thought having strong faith meant always waking up hopeful and certain. But looking back, I realize some of my truest moments of faith showed up when hope was nowhere to be found, when I felt empty, but decided to trust anyway.

Another moment hit during a season of financial strain. I remember opening the fridge late one night, staring at shelves that were almost empty. My faith felt as thin as the light in that refrigerator. Still, I stood there and started recalling all the times God had come through before. The groceries didn't magically appear the next morning, but something else did: peace. And that unexpected peace turned out to be exactly what I needed; it filled me up in ways a stocked fridge never could.

## Closing

Let your waiting season be where your roots grow deepest. When the storm hits, you may bend, but you won't break. The test of waiting is also the making of your faith; one honest, imperfect day at a time.

Faith roots you in the wait but roots alone don't sustain you. What keeps you breathing, day after day, is prayer. That's where we go next in Chapter Six: Prayer in the Wait.

## CHAPTER FIVE NOTES

**Reflection Pause**: Where has your faith felt fragile lately? What small choices could help you sink your roots deeper today?

# PHASE III — GUARDING

## PROTECTING YOUR HEART AND MIND DURING THE BATTLE OF WAITING.

# CHAPTER SIX
# Prayer in the Wait

## Why Prayer Feels Hard in Waiting

Prayer is supposed to be the lifeline of faith, but in waiting seasons, it often feels like the heaviest thing in the world. There were nights I cried out to God and wondered if my words were bouncing off the ceiling. I prayed the same prayer so many times it felt worn out, like a song stuck on repeat.

Sometimes prayer came easily, tears, groans, whispered words that spilled straight from the heart. At other times, it felt forced, like dragging words out of an empty well. And then there were days when silence felt safer than speaking, because I was tired of disappointment.

Prayer in the wait isn't polished. It's messy, repetitive, and sometimes desperate. It's not the kind you'd write neatly in a journal; it's the kind you cry in the dark when no one else hears. And that's the irony of waiting: the moments you need prayer the most are often when it feels the hardest to pray.

## My Adoption Prayers

Through those long years of waiting for my son, prayer changed shapes. Some days, I'd storm heaven with passionate pleas, begging God to speed up the process, to move paperwork off unknown desks and unlock doors that stayed stubbornly shut. Other days, my prayers lost their fire and shrank to tired whispers, "God, if this never happens, just help me make it through this longing."

Holidays stung the most. I'd find myself kneeling by the Christmas tree, hands clasped tight, asking for a miracle that never seemed to come. Each time I flipped a calendar page, it felt heavier in my hands, as if every unanswered prayer added a stone to the pile on my chest.

But here's the truth: Even on the days when all I could offer were broken, fragile prayers, barely more than a whisper, they were never ignored. God didn't tune me out. He was gathering up every single one, holding them close, weaving them quietly into His own timing.

## Prayer on the Move

In the Air Force, prayer became second nature. During long staff meetings that dragged on for hours, I would often find myself praying. Sitting in the back of a community-center classroom or standing in the grocery line, I prayed. Wherever I was, I found small spaces to talk to God, between tasks, between moments, and between breaths.

Sometimes those prayers were long and detailed; other times they were simple one-liners: *"Lord, keep us safe. "Lord, give me courage."*

Whether waiting for updates, working late, or sitting in yet another office while paperwork crawled, I prayed through it all. The pace of military life made prayer less about eloquence and more about endurance. That habit carried over into civilian life. Prayer in waiting doesn't have to be fancy; it just must be honest.

## Porchlight Prayers

Not every prayer happens in motion. Some rise in the stillness of night when the world finally quiets down.

My friend shared that she sat on her porch long after the day ended, the hum of crickets filling the silence, her Bible beside her, and her thoughts slow enough to finally listen. Streetlights flickered, the air felt thick with peace, and she whispered prayers that didn't need fancy words, just honesty.

Sometimes I'd walk the same neighborhood path again and again, the rhythm of my steps becoming its own kind of prayer. Other nights, I'd look up at the stars and feel small but seen, reminded that the same God who scattered constellations could still hear me whisper His name.

Those moments didn't bring quick answers, but they grounded me. They reminded me that prayer doesn't just move mountains, it steadies the heart that's waiting for them to move.

And maybe that's part of the gift of waiting, it slows you down enough to notice God in the quiet places you once rushed past.

## When Heaven Feels Silent

The silence of waiting makes prayer feel like it's going nowhere. You pour out your heart and get nothing back. You fast, plead, push, but heaven seems mute.

My friend told me about a season of being angry at God for not answering his prayers. He accused Him of ignoring him, of playing favorites, of being distant. Silence made him doubt God's goodness.

But later, he realized silence doesn't mean absence. Think of the caterpillar tucked away in a cocoon. It looks like nothing's happening from the outside, but inside, transformation is quietly taking place. In the same way, the silence of waiting is not proof of neglect; it's the space where something beautiful is being formed before it emerges.

## Prayer as Warfare

Paul urges us in Ephesians 6:18 (NIV) to "pray in the Spirit on all occasions with all kinds of prayers and requests." Prayer isn't just a quiet conversation; it's how we suit up for battle. While we wait, impatience, comparison, and weariness circle like enemies at the gate. Prayer is how we push back.

When impatience starts shouting, "You're running out of time," I respond with prayer, "My times are in His hands." When comparison whispers, "Look at everyone getting ahead of you," prayer reminds me, "God's plan for me is mine and mine alone." When weariness groans,

"You can't keep this up," prayer becomes my rallying cry, "His strength is made perfect in my weakness."

Prayer is warfare. It's how we keep standing moment by moment.

## Everyday Prayers

Prayer doesn't just happen on your knees in a quiet room. It often bursts out in the middle of life.

I once choked so badly I couldn't swallow. My prayer wasn't eloquent; it was one desperate cry: "God, help me breathe." Another time, after an accident left me with stitches in my head, I whispered prayers for strength on an ER table, trying not to pass out.

I've prayed while waiting for my laundry to finish at the laundromat, hoping I had enough quarters. I've prayed in unemployment offices, outside closed doors before an interview, and even while pacing the backyard as the sun set, trying to walk off my worries. None of those prayers was pretty or polished. But every one of them was real.

And prayer isn't always heavy. When my niece bought her first house, we prayed for everything to go smoothly, only to laugh when the first thing to break was the toilet. God has a sense of humor. God has a way of keeping prayer both serious and lighthearted, reminding me to keep talking to Him through it all.

## Biblical Anchors of Prayer in Waiting

Scripture is filled with stories of people who discovered the power of prayer while they waited.

**Cornelius prayed** faithfully even before he fully understood who God was. His prayers rose as a memorial before God and opened the door to revelation.

**Anna prayed** in the temple for decades, waiting to see the Messiah, and she did.

**Paul and Silas prayed** and sang while chained in prison, their voices rising before their freedom ever came.

Their stories remind us prayer isn't wasted, even when the wait is long. Prayer in waiting becomes the steady beat that keeps you from losing heart.

## Humor in Prayer

Prayer in waiting often takes an unexpectedly lighthearted turn. I've circled crowded parking lots, whispering, "Lord, just one open spot, right up front would be great," as if God were running valet service. I've sat on the couch during thunderstorms, hands clasped, bargaining for the Wi-Fi to hang in there so my video call wouldn't freeze on the world's most awkward frame. I've laid a hopeful hand on a sputtering washing machine and prayed under my breath, "Please, not today. My bank account can't take it."

A friend once told me she pleaded with God for a clear sign, only to look up and see a giant fast-food billboard. We laughed until we cried, realizing that sometimes God answers with a wink—or at least a little comic relief. Humor sneaks into our prayers and carries us when the wait feels heavy. Sometimes, laughter is the lifeline that keeps you afloat when despair tries to pull you under.

## What Prayer Produces in Waiting

Prayer in waiting produces intimacy. It transforms silence into a place where you can meet God. It produces endurance, giving you the strength to persevere when nothing seems to move. It produces peace, a calm that doesn't make sense on paper. And it fosters trust, the kind that endures even when the outcome is uncertain.

Prayer doesn't erase the ache, but it transforms it. Waiting shifts from feeling like punishment to becoming a season of preparation.

## My Breakthroughs in Prayer

My biggest breakthroughs in waiting didn't come when God changed my circumstances. They came when prayer changed me.

I realized what I really needed wasn't for God to move faster, but for Him to anchor me right where I was. I stopped begging for shortcuts and started asking for strength. Prayer stopped being about getting the answer I wanted and became about staying connected when answers were slow to come.

## Closing

Prayer in the wait isn't always pretty. Sometimes it's messy, raw, and repetitive. But every prayer matters. Every word, every sigh, every groan is heard by God. Waiting may silence your confidence, but it doesn't silence your prayers. They rise even when you don't feel them. And in time, you'll see prayer carry you through what you thought would break you.

Prayer grounds us in waiting, but what we pray for also needs protection. That's where we're headed next in Chapter Seven: Guarding in the Wait.

# CHAPTER SIX NOTES

**Reflection Pause:** Which expression of prayer, lament, thanksgiving, warfare, or silence do you need to lean into in this season?

## Chapter Seven

# Guarding in the Wait

## Why Guarding Matters

Waiting isn't passive; it's a fight. And if you've ever been in a long wait, you know exactly what I mean. The real struggle isn't only about the wait itself; it's about what the wait tries to steal from you, your peace, your hope, your focus, and your faith.

The longer you wait, the more vulnerable you feel. Discouragement slips in like a thief at night. Doubt whispers lies so convincing that you start to believe them. Comparison drains your joy as you scroll through everyone else's highlight reels. Distractions multiply until the trivial feels urgent and the important things slip through your hands.

Guarding is the difference between surviving the wait and being swallowed by it. Proverbs 4:23 (NIV) says, "Above all else, guard your heart, for everything you do flows from it." That's not just pretty poetry, that's survival advice. If you don't guard your heart in waiting, delay will turn into bitterness.

It's like boarding up a house in a storm. You can't stop the wind or the rain, but you can protect what's inside. Guarding doesn't remove the storm, but it keeps you standing through it. Waiting is the storm; guarding is the shield. Without it, the storm doesn't just hit you, it moves in and starts rearranging the furniture of your soul.

That's why Philippians 4:7 (NIV) reminds us, *"And the peace of God, which transcends all understanding, will guard your hearts and your minds in Christ Jesus."* Guarding isn't about control; it's about peace. The kind that keeps you steady when everything else shakes.

## Guarding in Everyday Life

Guarding usually shows up in small, everyday choices. It's the decision to stay patient when the ticket site keeps refreshing and you're tempted to give up. It's stepping back from conversations that drain your spirit. It's learning to say no to one more commitment, so you don't stretch yourself to the breaking point. And it's shutting down the endless scroll of bad news or comparison, so your mind has space to breathe.

One afternoon, I sat in a crowded waiting room where everyone kept glancing at the clock, restless and anxious for their names to be called. It struck me that guarding your peace works in a similar way; you can't control the timing, but you can decide what you focus on while you wait. Peace isn't found in faster answers; it's built in quieter focus.

Later, at an unemployment office with my son, where the system was crawling, the line was long, and the whole room felt heavy with frustration. Some people let that weight turn into anger, snapping at the workers, blaming themselves, or lashing out. We noticed one woman quietly guarding her peace. She stayed steady. She refused to let the bitterness around her take root. Guarding doesn't always look dramatic. Sometimes it looks like it is simply holding onto your dignity when everything around you feels humiliating.

I've seen it in builders too, laying foundation stone by stone, day after day. From the outside, progress seemed slow, even invisible. Doubt was loud, but guarding meant showing up anyway. Guarding meant trusting the unseen progress instead of letting discouragement derail the work.

Guarding in the wait looks less like building walls and more like building wisdom. It's not about ignoring the battle; it's about refusing to let discouragement or distraction steer the wheel.

## Guarding the Next Generation

Guarding doesn't stop with us. Kids today are bombarded with noise, social media, peer pressure, and endless comparisons. If waiting seasons leave adults vulnerable, imagine what they do to a child or teen who hasn't yet built resilience.

Guarding the next generation means teaching them how to filter what they see and hear. It's helping them understand that likes and followers don't equal worth. It's reminding them that silence from God doesn't mean absence. It's showing them that waiting isn't wasted, it's a training ground.

I mentored a teenager once who said, "I feel like I'm behind because all my friends already know what they want to do with their lives." At fifteen, she was already crushed under the weight of comparison. Guarding her heart meant speaking life into her, reminding her she was on her own timeline, not anyone else's.

Kids learn even more by watching us. If I say, "I'm trusting God," but spiral into stress at the first delay, what am I really teaching? They learn more from how we live our waiting than from anything we preach. Our guarded hope becomes their model of resilience.

And here's the bigger truth: the way we handle waiting teaches them how to handle theirs. If they see us collapse, they'll think that's the only way. But if they see us guard our peace, our joy, and our faith, they'll carry those tools into their own storms.

## Guarding in Practice

During my adoption wait, guarding my heart became a daily battle. Every Mother's Day felt like a fresh bruise. I'd see bouquets and cards in shop windows, and it was all I could do not to turn away. I learned to quietly skip certain gatherings, knowing that sometimes protecting my peace meant sitting out the celebrations. That wasn't weakness; it was learning when to step back so I didn't get swallowed up by sorrow.

The military hammered the concept of guarding into me, but in a different language. I remember sitting behind a desk, eyes scanning sensitive reports, double- and triple-checking every detail. There was no room for daydreaming; one distracted moment could mean a costly mistake, and sometimes, mistakes had real consequences. Guarding wasn't just about stacks of paperwork; it was about how you sat, how you listened, how you stayed ready, even when the world around you was spinning. That discipline followed me home, showing up in smaller ways, like paying attention to the thoughts I let linger, the words I spoke, and the peace I worked to protect.

## Biblical Anchors of Guarding

The Bible makes it clear: guarding isn't optional, it's essential. Nehemiah guarded the rebuilding of Jerusalem's wall with a sword in one hand and a trowel in the other. He knew distraction and opposition were as dangerous as any attack. Guarding wasn't about stopping the work; it was about protecting it from collapse.

Gideon guarded his army by letting God strip it down to 300 men. Guarding, in his case, wasn't about numbers; it was about trust. Less with God was stronger than more without Him.

Joshua reminded the people to meditate on God's word day and night. Guarding wasn't passive; it was an active focus, staying rooted in truth so battles couldn't shake them off course.

## Humor in Guarding

Guarding doesn't always feel brave; sometimes, it's downright absurd. I've declared a sugar-free "health reset," only to catch myself clutching a pint of chocolate fudge brownie ice cream like it was the last treasure on earth. I've told myself I'd just check my phone for a minute, and suddenly I'm deep into a string of funny toddler videos, wondering where the time went.

I've set up strict routines to protect my focus, only to find myself binge-watching shows and convincing myself it was "rest." I've carved out time to pray, only to get sidetracked scrubbing baseboards that hadn't seen attention in months. Guarding your life doesn't always look like winning. Sometimes, it looks like laughing at your own detours and giving yourself grace to try again tomorrow.

This is where humor steps in. Proverbs 17:22 (NIV) says, "A cheerful heart is good medicine." Sometimes laughter is a shield; it lightens the load just enough so despair doesn't get the upper hand.

## What Guarding Produces

When you guard your heart, mind, and spirit, something powerful happens. Guarding produces resilience, the strength to rise again when discouragement knocks you down. It produces clarity, helping you focus on what truly matters instead of getting lost in noise. It produces peace, a calm that doesn't erase the storm but lets you breathe inside it.

Guarding also sharpens discernment. You learn to separate truth from lies, urgent from important, temporary from eternal. Not every voice deserves attention. Not every invitation deserves a yes. Not every thought deserves space in your mind.

Most of all, guarding produces endurance. Waiting is a marathon, not a sprint. Guarding teaches you to pace yourself, to preserve your strength, and to keep hope alive. It won't shorten the wait, but it will keep you from burning out before the breakthrough comes.

## Closing

Guarding in the wait is a fight worth choosing. It's not glamorous, and it's rarely easy, but every guarded thought, every protected boundary, every moment you refuse to let discouragement take over is a victory. Waiting may strip away control, but guarding your heart keeps it intact.

Guarding may keep you standing, but sometimes waiting feels like a full-on battle. That's why the next step matters: Chapter Eight: Warring in the Wait.

# CHAPTER SEVEN NOTES

**Reflection Pause:** What's the hardest area for you to guard right now, your heart, your mind, your environment, or your habits?

# Chapter Eight

# Warring in the Wait

## The Battle Beneath the Surface

Waiting isn't just emotional, it's spiritual. Underneath the frustration, silence, and delay, there's a real war going on. And it's not only about what you're waiting for, but also about who you're becoming while you wait.

The enemy loves to plant lies during waiting seasons: *"God forgot you." "This will never happen." "You don't deserve it."* Those lies are sneaky. They slip in quietly, but if you don't push back, they start to take root. That's why waiting requires warfare, not the kind fought with noise and weapons, but the kind fought with prayer, truth, and perseverance.

You can't afford to be passive. If you don't fight for your peace, your hope, and your faith, the enemy will take them.

I've seen this play out in my own life, and I've seen it in others. A young athlete I knew was sidelined by an injury that kept him off the field for months. Every game he missed felt like confirmation of the lie: *"You'll never recover. You've lost your chance."* The battle wasn't just against the physical injury; it was against the despair, trying to convince him that his future was over. He had to learn to fight back with truth before he could step onto the field again with confidence.

That's the heart of warring in the wait. It's not just about the job, the healing, or the breakthrough. It's about refusing to let lies rewrite your story while you wait.

## Wrestling with Hope

On my adoption journey, I lived this battle daily. Silence stretched so long it echoed. Lies had time to build fortresses in my mind. I fought discouragement, whispering it was too late. I wrestled with bitterness as I saw other families gathering for milestones I was still waiting for. I fought despair on nights when my prayers met only quiet.

Warring in that wait meant refusing to surrender hope, even when it felt pointless. It meant speaking truth over myself when my emotions told me to quit. Some days, I fought with strength. Other days, my prayer was barely a whisper: "Lord, help me." But even whispers count as weapons when they're grounded in faith.

## Training for Resistance

Waiting feels a lot like stepping into an arena. Each morning, you lace up and face a fresh opponent, maybe it's exhaustion, maybe it's the voice that says you're falling behind, maybe it's the lure of giving up or the sting of envy watching someone else's win. Some days, you get in a good hit and feel strong. Other days, you're just dodging punches, doing your best to stay on your feet.

But every round, win or lose, teaches you how to get up and keep going.

The goal isn't to be flawless; it's to keep showing up. Endurance isn't built on the easy days; it's forged in the fight, one round at a time.

## Everyday Fights

You don't need a crisis for this kind of struggle to show up. Some of the toughest battles sneak in during the most ordinary moments.

I've fought it while lying in bed, eyes wide open, replaying conversations and wrestling with the thought that I'll never get it right. I've felt it flare up when I glance over at someone else's progress, quietly measuring my own timeline against theirs. Sometimes, it's as simple as watching my GPS reroute for the third time, sighing and thinking, "Figures, my life's in perpetual recalculating mode."

I see it in the lives around me, too. A young mom, waiting for childcare so she can return to work, wrestles with the fear that she's missing out or that important moments are slipping past her. A recent college grad, sending out résumé after résumé, faces a wall of rejections but keeps choosing persistence over despair. A father, hoping for reconciliation with his estranged son, carries on a private battle, fending off hopelessness while leaving the door open for forgiveness.

These struggles might not look dramatic to anyone else, but they demand real courage. Warring in the wait is about refusing to let fear, anxiety, or despair call the shots.

## Biblical Anchors of Warfare

Jacob spent an entire night wrestling with God, grappling in the dark, refusing to let go until he got a blessing. When morning broke, he walked away limping, marked by the struggle. His battle didn't break him; it became part of his story, marking him as someone changed by perseverance.

Jesus showed us how to fight through silence. In the wilderness, He faced down every temptation, not with fists or force, but with words of Scripture. Each time a lie was thrown His way, He answered with truth, holding His ground until the enemy finally backed down.

Paul painted life with God as a fight worth finishing. His victories weren't about comfort or applause, but about grit, enduring shipwrecks, prison cells, betrayals. He kept showing up, faith in hand, determined not to quit, no matter how rough the road became.

These stories remind us that warring in the wait isn't about big moments or putting on a show. It's about holding tight, especially when every part of you wants to let go.

"Finally, be strong in the Lord and in his mighty power. Put on the full armor of God, so that you can take your stand against the devil's scheme" Ephesians 6:10-11 (NIV).

## Humor in the Fight

Warfare in waiting isn't glamorous. It's gritty, unpredictable, and sometimes the only way to keep going is to laugh at yourself in the middle of it.

I once texted my prayer partner, "I'm fighting the good fight," but autocorrect decided I was "fighting the good flight." Honestly, maybe it wasn't wrong, because some days I'd rather run from the hard stuff than face it. It made me laugh out loud, and in that laugh, I realized even weariness has humor tucked inside it.

Then there was the gym day. I was halfway through a workout, praying for strength, when I realized God was giving it to me the hard way, through sore muscles and sweat I wanted to escape. As I groaned through push-ups, I muttered, "Lord, I meant *spiritual* strength, not upper-body." But perhaps that's how God trains us, body, mind, and spirit, building endurance where we least expect it.

That's the thing about warring in the wait. It doesn't always look polished or holy. Sometimes it looks like laughing through frustration and choosing to keep showing up anyway. God isn't grading you on how perfect your fight looks; He's honoring the fact that you're still in it.

## What Warring Produces

Warfare in waiting doesn't always change circumstances right away, but it always changes you. It sharpens your focus, deepens your faith, and builds resilience. You start to recognize lies more quickly and respond to them with truth instead of fear.

Think of Nelson Mandela, twenty-seven years behind bars, yet he appeared steady, not bitter, ready to lead. Or Dr. Martin Luther King Jr., who kept declaring hope even when progress felt impossibly slow. Their waiting seasons were battlefields, but perseverance turned their delay into destiny.

The enemy wants to break you. But when you choose to war instead of surrender, waiting becomes the place where your spirit is forged into something unshakable.

## Closing

Warring in the wait isn't about fighting for outcomes; it's about fighting for your faith. It's about refusing to let silence steal your hope or lies steal your peace. The battle beneath the surface is real, but so is the God who equips you.

Suit up. Keep fighting. Even your whispers count as weapons.

Warring in the wait strengthens your spirit, but it also clears the way for something deeper: fasting. Stripping away distractions makes the fight sharper. That's where we head in Chapter Nine: Fasting in the Wait.

# CHAPTER EIGHT NOTES

**Reflection Pause:** What lies are circling in your mind right now, the ones that whisper you're forgotten, unworthy, or too late?

_____
_____
_____
_____
_____
_____
_____
_____
_____
_____
_____
_____
_____
_____
_____
_____
_____
_____
_____
_____

# Phase IV-Glorifying

**PRAISE, FASTING, AND THANKSGIVING SHIFT YOUR POSTURE FROM FRUSTRATION TO FAITH.**

## Chapter Nine

# Fasting in the Wait

## Why Fasting Feels Like Too Much

Let's be real, if waiting already feels hard, fasting can feel like too much. You're already stretched thin, worn down from unanswered prayers, and now you're supposed to give something up? That's exactly how I felt for years. Fasting sounded extreme, even unnecessary.

Before we dive in, let me pause and say this: fasting is personal, and it's not one-size-fits-all. If you have health concerns, medical conditions, or take regular medication, talk with your doctor before starting any kind of food-related fast. There are plenty of other ways to fast, like stepping back from distractions, habits, or comforts, which may be safer for you in this season.

But here's what I've learned: fasting isn't about punishment, it's about sharpening. It strips away what numbs us, the things we run to when waiting gets heavy. It quiets distractions so we can hear God more clearly. In a waiting season, when life feels loud with frustration, fasting is one of the few things that pulls the volume down.

## My First Real Fast

I still remember my first attempt at a "real" fast. I figured it was mostly about skipping meals so God would pay extra attention. By day two, I was irritable, my head was throbbing, my stomach sounded like a wild animal, and my mind was fixated on fantasies of pepperoni pizza.

But somewhere in the middle of that weakness, something shifted. Fasting wasn't about what I was giving up; it was about what I was making space for. Every hunger pang nudged me to pray. Every craving turned into a reminder that my need for God ran deeper than my need for food. I didn't get a lightning-bolt answer, but I did walk away steadier, more focused, more trusting. The waiting didn't end, but I found a new strength inside it.

Even now, when I walk around the park in the evenings, the smell of someone else's dinner drifting through the air tempts me to give in. Yet even that moment is a lesson: discipline isn't just about what you set aside, but what you allow to fill you up. The air feels cleaner, my thoughts settle, and the hunger itself becomes a quiet kind of prayer. On those walks, I'm reminded that fasting is less about what's off your plate and more about what's filling your spirit.

That's the surprising part of fasting: it doesn't always move the mountains outside you, but it strengthens the ground beneath your feet.

## Fasting Beyond Food

Over time, I've seen fasting in various unexpected forms. Sometimes, God calls us to fast from the things that quietly drain us: habits, comforts, or distractions that keep us from hearing Him.

I knew a single mom who fasted from television. She admitted she was using endless episodes to numb her exhaustion. Instead, she carved out that time to journal prayers for her kids. That fast didn't change her circumstances overnight, but it gave her the focus she needed to keep going.

A co-worker fasted from complaining. Every time he wanted to vent about being laid off, he forced himself to write down something he was grateful for instead. By the time he landed a job months later, he had a whole notebook of gratitude that reminded him how God had carried him.

My cousin once fasted from shopping. Her child was in the hospital, and she realized she'd been coping with stress by swiping her card. Instead, she chose to break that habit by bringing her Bible into the waiting room instead of her laptop. She told me that the shift gave her peace she hadn't felt in months.

That's the thing about fasting: it's not a bargaining chip to twist God's arm. It's a way of grounding yourself, stripping away what numbs you so you can lean on what really sustains.

## Fasting as Strength Training

Fasting is less about sacrifice and more about building resilience. It teaches discipline, the art of saying "no" to cravings so you can say "yes" to God. And that discipline doesn't stay in the fast; it spills into every waiting season of life.

Think of a musician preparing for a performance. Long before stepping on stage, they practice scales, rehearse pieces, and repeat the same passages until their fingers know them by heart. Waiting for the concert requires the same kind of discipline fasting builds: small, daily choices that sharpen you for something greater.

I once heard of a college student waiting for exam results who fasted from television. She said, "I don't want to waste my mind on reruns. I want to sharpen it for what's ahead." Her fast didn't change the score report, but it changed her focus and gave her strength to prepare for the next step.

And I met a professor who fasted from multitasking. He realized he was living in constant motion, grading papers, answering texts, and half-listening to his students while thinking about the next task. His fast was simple: one thing at a time. He called it "slow obedience." It didn't shorten his workload, but it restored his peace of mind.

That's the hidden gift of fasting: it builds muscles you don't know you need until the waiting stretches longer than you imagined.

## Humor in Fasting

Let's be honest, fasting has its own brand of humor. The minute you swear off sugar, it seems like every other commercial is a slow-motion close-up of donuts. As soon as you log off social media, you're convinced your phone is buzzing in your pocket, even when it's across the room. My cousin tried fasting from coffee once and suddenly realized every coffee shop in town was advertising half-off caramel lattes.

Fasting has a way of revealing just how much your cravings run the show, and how absurd you can get when you're trying to ignore them. Maybe that's part of the lesson. You end up laughing at your own antics while you learn what real dependence looks like. A little humor goes a long way when the sacrifice feels heavy; sometimes, it's the laughter that keeps you steady.

## Biblical Anchors of Fasting

From Genesis to Revelation people turned to fasting during their hardest waits.

Moses climbed the mountain and went without food for forty days, holding out for God's instructions, his hunger echoing the longing for direction. Esther called her community to fast before she risked everything to save her people; her empty stomach matched her courage. Even Jesus Himself spent forty days in the wilderness, fasting before stepping into His ministry, letting hunger carve out space for something greater.

These fasts weren't about trying to look holy. They were about preparation. Each story shows how fasting took raw desperation and turned it into the strength needed for the next step. The wait wasn't erased, but endurance grew in the quiet hunger.

## What Fasting Produces in Waiting

Fasting isn't about trying to convince God to see things our way or accelerate an answer. Instead, it's about letting God transform us in the process of waiting.

**It produces humility.** A skipped meal reminds you how fragile your strength really is, but it also points you to the One who never runs out.

**It produces clarity.** Cutting away clutter helps you see what actually matters.

**It produces perseverance.** Saying "no" to small cravings trains you to endure bigger battles.

**It produces dependence**. Each hunger pang, each craving, becomes a reminder that if God can sustain you in this sacrifice, He can sustain you in the larger waits as well.

That's what fasting does: it doesn't shorten the wait, but it strengthens you for it.

## My Breakthroughs in Fasting

Some of my biggest breakthroughs in waiting didn't come through answered prayers; they came through fasting.

One time, I gave up television for a month. The first week felt unbearable. Nights stretched long, and silence pressed in. But slowly, that quiet became space. I picked up my journal again. I started writing prayers instead of drowning my thoughts in background noise. That fast didn't bring a breakthrough in circumstances, but it brought one in me.

Another time, I fasted from over-planning. I'd been micromanaging every outcome, convinced I could schedule my way out of uncertainty. So I stopped. No lists, no color-coded timelines, just trust. It was harder than skipping meals, but that space made room for peace I hadn't felt in years. The answers didn't rush in, but the anxiety eased its grip.

Fasting taught me that a breakthrough doesn't always look like doors flying open. Sometimes it looks like standing strong until the door finally does.

## Closing

Fasting in the wait isn't about punishment; it's about preparation. It's about surrendering what you lean on so you can lean more fully on God. It won't always shorten the wait, but it will strengthen you in it.

Waiting strips away comfort. Fasting invites you to find your comfort in Him alone.

Fasting strips away distractions, but it also heightens the battle. When you fast, the fight sharpens. That's why the next phase matters: learning to war in the wait. Chapter Ten takes us there: Praise in the Wait.

# CHAPTER NINE NOTES

**Reflection Pause:** What distractions might God be inviting you to fast from: food, social media, shopping, busyness, entertainment?

# Chapter Ten

# Praise in the Wait

## Why Praise Feels Out of Place in Waiting

Here's the thing: praise is not the first thing that comes to mind when you're stuck in a waiting season. When the days feel endless and it seems like nothing you're hoping for is happening. Frustration? That makes sense. Complaints? Totally normal. Tears? Absolutely. But praise? That feels backward.

Why lift your hands when your heart feels heavy? Why sing when silence screams louder than any song? That's the beauty of praise; it doesn't ignore the pain; it shifts your focus towards hope.

Praise is not about pretending everything is fine. It's declaring that God is still faithful even when life isn't fair. It's not about feelings, it's about where you choose to stand. Waiting for tests that require choices like not complaining and comparing come naturally. Praise takes intention. It's resistance wrapped in gratitude.

## A Flat Tire and a Song

One night, after a long and exhausting day, I was driving home when my tire blew. A loud pop, a wobble, and suddenly I was stranded on the shoulder of a dark road.

Angry tears welled up. I didn't have the money for another tire. I didn't have the patience for one more problem to be added to the pile.

As I waited for roadside help, a praise song drifted through the radio. At first, I wanted to shut it off. What did singing have to do with this mess? But then, something in me softened. I started humming along. By the time the tow truck arrived, nothing about my situation had changed, but something in me had.

Praise hadn't fixed the flat, but it had lifted the weight. That night taught me something: praise doesn't fix everything, but it keeps despair from fixing itself to you.

## Praise as Resistance

Over time, I've realized that praising while you wait isn't just a spiritual exercise; it's a quiet rebellion. Every time you choose to praise, you're pushing back against fear, despair, and hopelessness. Praise refuses to surrender.

When fear creeps in and hisses, "You're finished," praise answers right back, "My story isn't over yet." When comparison pokes at you, "You should be further along by now, "praise gently reminds, "I'm exactly where I'm supposed to be." When despair settles in and sighs,

"None of this matters," praise insists, "Even this has meaning."

Praise doesn't let the enemy hold the pen. It's not pretending the struggle isn't real—it's standing your ground and declaring, "I won't let anything else write the ending."

## Everyday Anchors of Praise

Praise doesn't only belong in churches or on stages. It sneaks into the ordinary moments if you let it.

I've whispered thanks for sunrise after long nights, hummed hymns while folding laundry, and thanked God for heat when winter power failed.

I've seen a rise in others. A single father lifting his hands in church, even though bills were stacked high at home. A woman whispering praise during chemotherapy, not because she felt strong but because she knew where her strength came from. Their praise wasn't polished or pretty; it was a matter of survival.

Those small, ordinary moments didn't solve their waits, but they reminded them that even in the hard places, they weren't alone. That's what praise does: it breathes strength into weakness and anchors hope in the middle of real life.

One morning at a city park, I met an older groundskeeper who had worked there for decades. Every day, before the crowds arrived, he swept walkways while humming worship songs. He told me, 'I praise God before the noise starts, gratitude keeps the day from owning me.' His quiet joy reminded me that praise doesn't have to be loud to be powerful; it can rise from simple, faithful routines done with a thankful heart.

## A Teacher Who Chose Praise

I sat next to a woman at church who was a teacher during a particularly challenging time. Budget cuts, overcrowded classrooms, and personal illness, it felt like everything was pressing against her at once. She could have collapsed under it all, but instead she chose praise.

Every morning, before her students arrived, she walked the classroom whispering, "Thank You for these desks. Thank You for these children. Thank You for another day." Those simple words became her lifeline. The stress didn't vanish. The problems didn't go away. But her perspective shifted. She said her classroom felt less like a burden and more like an altar.

That's what praise does: it reframes. It doesn't always remove the weight, but it changes how you carry it.

## Biblical Anchors of Praise in Waiting

David had a whole book of praise and if you look, you will find many other chapters of people who chose praise before they ever saw a breakthrough.

Jehoshaphat sent singers ahead of the army to lead with gratitude before the battle was won. Habakkuk declared, "Though the fig tree does not bud and there are no grapes on the vines... yet I will rejoice in the Lord (3:17-18, NIV)." Job, after devastating loss, still found words of praise in his grief. He said, "The Lord gave and the Lord has taken away; may the name of the Lord be praised" (1:21, NIV).

None of them waited for everything to make sense before lifting their voices. They didn't praise after the miracle; they praised before it. That's what makes biblical praise so powerful: it's not reactive, it's prophetic. It speaks faith while the dust is still settling.

These weren't moments of triumph; they were moments of delay, fear, and loss. And yet, praise rose anyway.

## Humor in Praise

Praise definitely has its lighter moments.

I've thanked God for remembering my umbrella, only to realize it was still waiting by the front door as the rain started. There was the time I cranked up my favorite worship song in the living room, so loud my neighbor texted to ask if I was auditioning for a reality show. A friend once told me she offered a prayer of praise when her printer finally spat out a report without jamming, because she'd lost too many battles with temperamental technology.

Praise doesn't always show up as polished worship. Sometimes it's about laughing at your own forgetfulness, grinning at the little wins, or singing off-key at the top of your lungs when no one else is listening. Maybe that's exactly the point: praise doesn't need to be perfect. It just needs to be real.

## The Hardest Praise

But let's not sugarcoat it, some praise is born out of heartbreak.

I remember visiting a friend just after she'd lost her child. I braced myself for silence or anger, not knowing what to expect. But when I walked in, I heard her softly singing through her tears. Her voice was shaky, her face streaked with grief, but she kept going, refusing to let pain steal her song. That wasn't the polished kind of praise you hear on Sunday mornings. It was raw, trembling, and fragile, yet somehow, it was also the strongest praise I've ever seen.

That scene is etched in my memory. Praise in seasons of waiting isn't about acting like you're fine. It's about lifting your gaze, even when every part of you wants to fold in on itself.

## What Praise Produces

Praise doesn't take the pain away, but it lightens the weight of it. It gently redirects your gaze from everything that hasn't happened yet to the good that's still holding steady right now. Every simple song, every quiet "thank You," becomes a small act of resistance, pushing back against despair. Praise brings peace that defies logic and joy that slowly grows stronger each time you choose it.

That's the quiet strength of praise: it anchors you when silence feels suffocating. It won't turn waiting into a celebration, but it hands your voice back when life feels too heavy to sing. Praise doesn't fix everything, but it keeps you from coming undone while you wait.

## My Breakthroughs in Praise

One breakthrough showed up on a day when trust felt impossible. I remember sitting in my car, staring at the gas gauge pinned to empty, panic making my hands shake. Out of sheer desperation, I put on a worship playlist and started sorting through my checkbook, tears blurring the numbers. The math didn't change, but somewhere between the songs and the sobs, my heart did. Slowly, the panic loosened its grip.

Another breakthrough came after a tense conflict at work. My first urge was to fire off a sharp reply, but instead I slipped on my headphones and walked out into the cold night. Worship music filled my ears as the chill cleared the anger from my chest, and the lyrics softened what pride had hardened. The situation didn't magically resolve, but praise made me softer, steadier, and able to handle it differently.

As Paul wrote, "Let the peace of Christ rule in your hearts... and be thankful... singing to God with gratitude in your hearts" (Colossians 3:15–17, NIV). Praise is gratitude set to music; it's how you keep hope breathing when life feels tight.

## Closing

Praise doesn't magically cause the struggle to vanish. It doesn't fast-forward the clock. But it transforms how you live inside the delay. Praise says: I am not powerless. I am not abandoned. I still have a reason to sing.

Waiting may strip comfort, but praise keeps your soul alive. It reminds you that sorrow and joy can coexist, that hope and longing can stand together, and that your voice still matters even when your prayers feel unanswered.

Praise strengthens your spirit, but waiting doesn't end with a song. The journey continues to test you, with mistakes, setbacks, and detours. That's why the next chapter matters: Mistakes and Setbacks in the Wait.

## CHAPTER 10 NOTES

**Reflection Pause**: Where does praise feel out of place in your life right now? Can you imagine what it would look like to practice it anyway, even if it feels unnatural?

# Chapter Eleven

# Mistakes and Setbacks in the Wait

## When the Wait Gets Messy

Waiting seasons almost never unfold like a tidy storybook. They twist and turn, full of roadblocks you never saw coming, opportunities that fall apart at the last minute, disappointments that knock the wind out of you, endless detours that wear your patience thin. And the chaos isn't just out there; sometimes it's swirling inside, too. Some storms blow in from nowhere, but other times, you can trace the mess right back to your own choices.

Setbacks show up as doors slammed in your face, plans collapsing overnight, or storms rolling through just as you thought you had things figured out. Mistakes sneak in through impatience, decisions made when you're exhausted or scared, words that slip out before you think, risks you leap into too quickly, shortcuts that end up costing you more than you bargained for.

All together, it's easy to look at the wreckage and wonder if you've completely blown your chance.

But here's what I've learned, sometimes the hard way: mistakes and setbacks might slow your steps, but they don't take you out of the running. They don't erase what God is building in your story. If you let them, they become some of the sharpest, most honest teachers you'll ever have.

## My Breakthrough with Mistakes and Setbacks

One of the most challenging setbacks I faced happened during the Texas winter storm. In a single week, pipes burst, power failed, and the cold crept into every corner of the house. That storm wasn't my mistake; it was life happening in the worst way. But the aftermath forced me into a kind of waiting I never wanted, waiting for repairs, waiting for power, waiting for warmth. And yet, in that frozen stretch, I learned how to lean on God and on others in ways I never had before.

However, some of the waiting lessons came from my own doing. I once rushed a financial decision, signing too quickly because I couldn't stand the silence any longer. It cost me peace and years of strain, but it also taught me something priceless: never confuse speed with progress. Pray longer. Ask for counsel. Slow down before stepping in.

I've watched others navigate their own kinds of setbacks: a single mom rebuilding after a job loss, a friend recovering from a business deal that fell apart. Different details, same truth: both the storms we face and the stumbles we create can still shape us. Neither is wasted; both carve lessons that guide us forward.

## The Sting of Mistakes

Mistakes in waiting almost always have impatience at their root. You want something to happen so badly, you'll reach for whatever's closest, even when you know deep down it isn't right.

Maybe you've found yourself jumping into a friendship just to fill the silence, even though you sensed it wasn't healthy. Maybe you've blurted something out in a meeting and watched a bridge burn you wished you could rebuild. I've filled up my cart with things I couldn't afford and swiped my credit card, just to quiet the ache of feeling left out. The rush of relief vanished quickly, but the regret stuck around.

I've watched this play out in others, too. There was a single dad who hurried through paperwork, hoping to speed things up, only to get stuck in even more delays. An entrepreneur, eager to get moving, signed a contract without reading the fine print and spent years untangling the mess. A student, certain there was plenty of time, missed an application deadline by a single day. Mistakes like these happen to all of us; they're reminders of just how human we are when the waiting gets too heavy.

## The Weight of Setbacks

If mistakes sting, setbacks can feel like they knock the wind right out of you. These aren't messes you made yourself; they're losses that land on your doorstep without warning, demanding to be carried whether you're ready or not.

I've watched setbacks leave people reeling:

A caregiver, shoulders slumped, moving through another long day of tending to a loved one whose illness never lets up, exhaustion etched into every line of her face.

A factory worker, lunch pail in hand, clocking in day after day after half his crew was let go, each shift wondering if his name would be called next.

A small-business owner, unlocking her shop every morning, eyes glued to her phone, hoping for that long-awaited loan approval to finally come through—a breakthrough always just out of reach.

A soldier, boots polished and gear packed, living in limbo while waiting for deployment orders, heartbeat steady but mind always bracing for the call.

These are the storms you never saw coming. They bruise deep, rattle your confidence, and can make you question whether the waiting is even worth it. But as the storm rages, you start to see what really anchors you, what holds fast when everything else gets swept away.

## Biblical Anchors for Setbacks and Mistakes

The Bible doesn't hide failure; it highlights it.

**Peter swore he'd never deny Jesus**, but in one night, fear had him crumbling three times. Yet Jesus restored him and entrusted him with leading the church.

**Jonah ran in the opposite direction from God's call**, only to find himself in the belly of a fish. Yet God gave him another chance, and his reluctant obedience sparked revival.

**David's sin with Bathsheba carried consequences** that lasted the rest of his life, yet God still called him a man after His own heart.

Their stories remind me, and maybe you, that mistakes and setbacks don't cancel God's plans. If anything, they become the soil where grace grows deeper.

## Humor in the Mess

Not every mistake or setback ends in tears. Some of them, once the sting fades, turn into stories you can't help but laugh about later.

I've charred dinner so badly that the smoke alarm screeched for mercy and the whole house smelled like a campfire for days. I've walked into offices, head held high, only to realize I was a whole week early for my appointment. I've confidently pulled into the wrong driveway, waved enthusiastically at strangers, and only realized halfway through my wave that I'd never met them before.

A friend once hit "reply all" on a frustrated work email and immediately wanted to crawl under his desk and disappear. At the moment, these blunders felt mortifying. But looking back, they remind us not to take ourselves too seriously. Even when you're stuck in a long season of waiting, a sense of humor can soften the edges of your mistakes. Sometimes, grace is as simple as letting yourself smile at how wonderfully human you are.

## What Mistakes and Setbacks Produce

The very things that feel like they'll break you often end up building you.

Setbacks build muscle. Like scar tissue after an injury, each time you get back up, you prove you can bend without breaking. That's how resilience forms, not in comfort, but in the aftermath of recovery.

Mistakes slow you down and force reflection. They encourage you to pray longer, think more deeply, and listen more attentively before acting. Wrong turns, while costly, often redirect you onto better paths.

Together, setbacks and mistakes soften your heart. Once you've stumbled yourself, it's harder to judge the person lying face down. Compassion grows in the soil of failure.

And maybe most of all, they produce perspective. Setbacks remind you how little control you actually have; mistakes remind you how much grace you actually need. Both shift your focus from "I have to hold it all together" to "God is holding me together."

Philippians 1:6 (NIV) says, *"Being confident of this, that he who began a good work in you will carry it on to completion until the day of Christ Jesus."*

That verse reminds me that God's not done with me yet. Even in setbacks and self-inflicted detours, His work keeps moving forward, unfinished, but unstoppable.

They don't shorten the wait, but they deepen it, layering humility, endurance, compassion, and wisdom into your story.

## Closing

Waiting will always test you, and sometimes it will trip you, through no fault of your own or through choices you regret. But neither mistakes nor setbacks get to define your finish line.

They're detours, not dead ends. They bruise, but they don't bury. They might make the road longer, but they can also make it richer, filled with lessons you couldn't have learned any other way.

Your mistakes and setbacks are part of the story, but they are not the whole story. And they are never the end.

Setbacks and mistakes test your strength, but they also prepare you for what comes next. Once you've stumbled and got back up, you're ready for the next weapon in waiting: gratitude. That's where we head in Chapter Twelve: Thanksgiving in the Wait.

# CHAPTER ELEVEN NOTES

**Reflection Pause:** What setbacks have knocked you off course lately? What mistakes have weighed on you?

# CHAPTER TWELVE

# Thanksgiving as a Weapon

## Gratitude That Fights Back

By now, we've talked about thanksgiving as a posture in waiting, but let me take it a step further: thanksgiving isn't simply good manners or a pleasant thought. It's a weapon you wield.

Waiting can feel like a war zone. Doubt sneaks in quietly. Fear turns up the volume, drowning out what you know is true. Complaints feel natural, and bitterness is always ready to settle in. But thanksgiving? That's resistance in action. When you whisper "thank You" into the silence, you're not just trying to stay positive; you're drawing a line in the sand. Gratitude is rebellion against hopelessness.

It doesn't mean you suddenly feel cheerful or that your problems vanish overnight. It means you're standing your ground and refusing to let waiting rob you of your outlook. That choice carries real power.

Paul wrote it this way: "Rejoice always, pray continually, give thanks in all circumstances" (1 Thessalonians 5:16–18, NIV). Not after the blessing arrives. Not when the wait is finally over. Right in the thick of the ache, that's where thanksgiving turns into your fiercest weapon.

## My Adoption Weapon

While waiting for my adoption reunion, I learned just how sharp that weapon could be.

There were days when bitterness nearly swallowed me whole. I was jealous of other families and exhausted from disappointment. Some days, I didn't want to be thankful. Honestly, I wanted to scream. But I started forcing myself to thank God anyway, sometimes aloud in the car, sometimes scribbled in a journal.

And here's the surprising part: the circumstances didn't change. I was still waiting. But strength quietly took root where frustration once lived. The grip of despair loosened. Gratitude became oxygen when the wait tried to suffocate me. It wasn't natural; it felt more like dragging my soul into a fight. But that's the point. Thanksgiving in waiting isn't a mood. It's combat.

## Military Gratitude and Morale

The military gave me another picture of this. Gratitude worked like morale fuel. Entire units could shift just because someone chose to give thanks instead of grumble.

On long deployments, we had to thank God for everything. We were still tired and homesick, but we thanked Him for the small things. Mail from home. A working generator. A hot meal instead of rations.

Those thanks became shields against discouragement. Gratitude didn't erase the hardship, but it kept hope alive. Sometimes that was the difference between making it through the day or not.

## Everyday Weapons of Gratitude

Thanksgiving doesn't always show up as some big, dramatic gesture. More often, it's quiet and unassuming, woven into the small ways we serve and pay attention.

There's a retired coach I know who still shows up at the youth center, handing out water bottles and words of encouragement. He calls it his "thank-you shift." Watching him, I realize gratitude doesn't fade with age; it simply finds new ways to spill out.

I've whispered thanks for an old car that kept running when my bank account said otherwise. I've thanked God for laughter with a friend on days when loneliness pressed in. I've even been grateful for a warm mug of tea on mornings when I wasn't sure I'd make it through. Those little "thank Yous" might seem insignificant, but they land like punches against despair.

I see it in others, too. An artist waiting to hear if her work would be accepted into a gallery told me she'd started thanking God every morning, not for a "yes," but for the courage to keep painting. "If I can still pick up a brush," she said, "I have something to be grateful for."

A restaurant server who lost her job during a shutdown told me she thanked God every morning for the food still on her table. "I've lost my paycheck," she said, "but I haven't lost my family." Gratitude became the one thing unemployment couldn't touch.

That's the quiet miracle of thanksgiving in the wait: it doesn't erase delays, but it shifts the weight. It moves you from being crushed beneath it to finding just a little more room to breathe.

## Why Gratitude Feels Weak but Isn't

Here's the tricky thing: in the middle of waiting, gratitude can feel weathered, like an old tree that's stood through too many storms. What good is "thank You" when the bills are still due, the diagnosis hasn't changed, or the prayers feel unanswered?

I used to think gratitude was soft, something polite people practiced to smooth over rough edges. But I've learned it's anything but weak. Gratitude is gritty. It takes more strength to say "thank You" in the dark than to shout complaints in the light.

I think of a woman I met, standing in a housing office line for hours while paperwork decided whether she had a place to live. She whispered thanks that she still had friends to stay with that week. From the outside, it might have looked like denial. But for her, it was a matter of survival.

Or a community volunteer who spent months organizing food drives while waiting for her own job to come through. She said, "Serving others kept me from sinking. Gratitude was my anchor." Her thankfulness wasn't weathered; it was steady, seasoned, and strong.

Gratitude may not shout, but in waiting, it stands its ground.

Gratitude may look weak. But in waiting, it's often the strongest thing in the room.

## When Gratitude Feels Forced

Sometimes gratitude feels fake. You say "thank You" through clenched teeth, more out of obligation than genuine joy. I've been there. Writing lists when I didn't feel thankful. Whispering prayers that sounded hollow even to me.

But I've learned that forced gratitude still counts. It's like exercise on the days you don't want to move. Those are often the workouts that build the most strength. Gratitude works the same way. Some days you don't start with fireworks, you start with stubbornness.

A widow I met at church started writing one thank-you note a day. To people in a nursing home. To her doctor. Even to the clerk at the grocery store. She admitted it felt ridiculous at first. But over time, that practice rewired her. By the time new friendships began to form, she said, gratitude had changed her more than anything else could.

Sometimes gratitude doesn't start as a feeling. It starts as a decision. The feelings catch up later.

## Gratitude as Resistance

Gratitude is more than a mood; it's resistance. It pushes back against the pull of despair.

A writer once told me his book proposal was rejected three times. He said, "Every no feels like dying a little," but then he added, "If I let bitterness win, I'll still be locked inside even if someone finally says yes." His weapon was gratitude. After every rejection, he forced himself to write down three things for which he could still be thankful to God. "I'm still learning. I still have stories to tell. I can still write.

Resistance doesn't always look like protests or shouting. Sometimes it looks like a quiet "thank You" whispered in the dark.

## Humor in Gratitude

Not every thank-you is deep. Some are downright funny.

I've thanked God out loud when the dryer finally finished without eating another sock, like it was a holy miracle. I've thanked Him when gas prices dropped by five cents, as if I'd won the lottery. I've even thanked Him for the last slice of pie, clutching it like divine provision.

Silly as they sound, those little thanks trained my heart. They reminded me not to take life or myself so seriously. Humor makes gratitude sharper because it sneaks up on despair and undercuts it with joy.

## Biblical Anchors of Thanksgiving in Waiting

The Bible ties thanksgiving directly to warfare.

**Paul and Silas prayed and sang hymns** at midnight in a prison cell, and the chains didn't just fall off them but off every prisoner listening. Their gratitude turned a jailhouse into a place of freedom.

**David poured out thanksgiving** in the Psalms, not from a palace but from caves, hiding places, and battlefields. His gratitude wasn't reserved for comfort; it was his weapon in the middle of fear.

**Jesus, hours before His arrest, took bread, broke it, and gave thanks.** He knew betrayal and the cross were coming, but His weapon was gratitude.

Even Revelation describes heaven's battle scenes filled with thanksgiving. Worship and gratitude aren't afterthoughts; they're weapons.

## What Thanksgiving Produces

Thanksgiving in the midst of quiet waiting build courage. It's what helps you get out of bed and keep showing up, even when despair whispers, "Just give up." It clears the fog, bringing back memories of the ways God has come through before, and nudging you to believe He'll do it again. Gratitude teaches you to lean on what's already in your hands, instead of losing sleep over what's missing. And it grows a kind of joy that's deeper than surface happiness, the kind that anchors you when life starts to shake.

That's the power of gratitude: it changes your posture in the waiting. It helps you lift your gaze when everything around you feels heavy. It steadies your heart, even when you have no idea how things will turn out.

Thanksgiving doesn't shorten the wait, but it gives you solid ground to stand on while you're in it.

## My Breakthroughs in Gratitude

My biggest breakthrough came when I stopped waiting for gratitude to feel natural. I realized I could wield it even when my emotions didn't agree. Another came when I began using gratitude in prayer like armor. Instead of begging endlessly, I started thanking God in advance. "Thank You for hearing me. Thank You that You're working even when I don't see it. Thank You that the wait won't be wasted."

Those prayers didn't unlock doors overnight, but they gave me solid ground to stand on. Gratitude became the shield I leaned on when everything else felt shaky.

## Closing

Gratitude in waiting is more than a polite gesture. It's a weapon. Every "thank You" is a strike against the lies that say you're forgotten, hopeless, or alone. Gratitude doesn't erase the ache, but it fights back against the darkness.

When you choose thanksgiving in the silence, you're not just surviving the wait; you're warring with hope.

Thanksgiving sharpens your spirit, but waiting doesn't end there. The final step is what you do with the strength you've gained, how you pay it forward. That's where we're headed in Chapter Thirteen: Paying It Forward in the Wait.

## CHAPTER TWELVE NOTES

**Reflection Pause:** Where could thanksgiving become a weapon in your waiting season?

## Chapter Thirteen
# Paying It Forward in the Wait

## Why Paying It Forward Matters

Waiting has a way of making you turn inward. You start noticing every ache, every dream still on hold, every prayer that seems to go unanswered. Your thoughts get stuck in a loop. When will it be my turn? Why not me? And as the silence stretches out, it's easy to become wrapped up in your own longing.

But here's the unexpected gift waiting sometimes hands you: even when you feel empty, there's still something inside worth giving. Paying it forward doesn't wipe away the ache, but it gently shifts your gaze outward. Instead of circling what hasn't happened yet, you start to notice the ways you can bless someone else with what you already have, maybe it's a kind word, a story of your own experience, a little extra empathy, or simply showing up when it matters. It's a quiet way of saying, my waiting won't just change me; it can reach someone else, too.

## Giving from the Weight

During the long stretch of my adoption journey, generosity wasn't easy. Most days, I felt worn down, stretched thin, and unsure how much more I could give. But the moments I chose to give anyway ended up being the ones that brought the most healing.

I mentored women navigating the adoption journey, even though I hadn't yet experienced my own breakthrough. I shared honestly with people who felt invisible. I donated to family-support ministries even while I was longing for my own. None of that erased the strain, but it reminded me that I still had something valuable inside me, perspective and compassion.

Paying it forward doesn't mean the struggle disappears; it means it gets re-purposed. It turns private pain into connection and strength.

## Serving While Waiting

The military taught me early that waiting doesn't mean doing nothing. Flights were delayed, paperwork stalled, but there was always work to do in the meantime. Clean equipment. Train new recruits. Check supplies. Encourage morale.

That mindset carried into my everyday life. Just because your dream job hasn't opened doesn't mean you can't develop your craft. Just because your prayer hasn't been answered doesn't mean you can't speak life into someone else's situation. Paying it forward gives purpose to the pause. It keeps your spirit moving when life feels stagnant.

## Everyday Acts of Paying It Forward

Generosity doesn't need to be grand. Most of the time, it shows up in small, ordinary ways.

I've seen a restaurant server who barely made rent still tip the busboy extra at the end of her shift. A city bus driver keeps candy in his pocket to hand to kids getting on after school, he says it reminds him that kindness costs almost nothing.

A warehouse worker helped a new employee learn the ropes even though she was competing for the same promotion.

A retired veteran volunteers to fix bikes for neighborhood kids because he remembers not being able to afford one himself.

These aren't headline acts. They're small sparks of good that travel farther than we imagine.

In my own waiting seasons, I cooked meals when I was bone-tired. I prayed for other people's breakthroughs while still waiting on mine. I told my unpolished stories so someone else wouldn't feel like a failure. Each act reminded me that waiting can still bear fruit if I'm willing to plant something.

## Stories of Generosity in the Wait

My niece spent months hoping for a college acceptance letter that never arrived. Instead of letting disappointment swallow her, she found herself tutoring younger students who struggled with math. She told me it kept her steady, reminding her that, even when her own future felt uncertain, she could still pour something good into someone else's life.

I once met a grocery clerk who'd lost his home in a fire. When I asked how he stayed hopeful, he smiled and said, "Every shift, I pick one customer and try to make them laugh. If I can do that, the day's a win." He was quietly rebuilding his world, one small kindness at a time.

And generosity has a way of growing. In Houston Texas, a group of regulars pooled their tips to help a waitress whose car had broken down. Word got around, and by the end of the week, strangers from all over the city had chipped in enough to cover the repairs. That one simple act set off a chain reaction of hope that reached far beyond a single restaurant.

You don't need millions to make a difference. Sometimes, your listening ear, a little of your time, or a genuine smile are the most valuable gifts you can give, and they multiply every time you offer them.

## Humor in Paying It Forward

Not every act of kindness goes off without a hitch. I once tried to pay for the car behind me in a drive-thru, picturing a small, kind gesture, only to discover I'd chosen the minivan carting an entire soccer team. My "little act of generosity" nearly maxed out my debit card, but the surprise on the cashier's face was worth every penny.

After a storm, my cousin decided to bake muffins for her neighbors. Half of them came out of the oven looking more like deflated pancakes than muffins, but she delivered them anyway. The laughter and smiles that followed were sweeter than anything she could have planned.

That's the beauty of paying it forward: it doesn't need to be perfect or get a standing ovation. It just needs a willing heart.

## Biblical Anchors of Paying It Forward

You can spot the generosity of waiting all throughout Scripture.

**Ruth, grieving and unsure of her future, chose to work the fields** alongside Naomi, her simple acts of care and loyalty quietly paving the way for redemption neither of them could have predicted.

**Dorcas sat with her needle and thread, sewing** garments for widows, long before anyone thought to thank her or tell her story.

**And Jesus, on the brink of His own suffering, knelt and washed** His disciples' feet, offering them dignity and love when He had every right to seek comfort Himself.

These stories are reminders that giving while you wait is never wasted. It plants seeds of hope in the very places where despair once tried to take root.

"Let us not become weary in doing good, for at the proper time we will reap a harvest if we do not give up" Galatians 6:9 (NIV).

## What Paying It Forward Produces

Generosity in waiting produces perspective; it widens your lens beyond your delay.

**It builds empathy**. Once you've chosen to give from your own struggle, your heart softens toward others' pain.

**It brings joy**, a quiet contentment that sneaks in when you serve despite the strain.

**It strengthens endurance**. Every time you give while empty, you prove waiting hasn't broken you.

**And it leaves a legacy**, acts of kindness ripple into generations you'll never see.

Most of all, paying it forward keeps resentment from hardening you. It turns waiting from a holding cell into a classroom where compassion is practiced daily.

## My Breakthroughs in Paying It Forward

One breakthrough came when I realized that paying it forward wasn't just for others, but for me as well. Every time I gave, I broke the spiral of self-pity. Every time I encouraged someone else, discouragement lost its grip on me.

Another came when someone told me how my story about waiting gave them the courage to face their own. My heartache became their encouragement. That's the mystery of God; He never wastes even the unfinished chapters of our stories.

## Closing

Paying it forward while waiting doesn't mean pretending you're fine. It means letting your pain become fuel for kindness. It means refusing to let delay shrink you into self-focus and instead allowing it to stretch you into generosity.

Your wait may not be over, but your impact doesn't have to wait. Somewhere, someone is praying for the very encouragement you already carry.

This is the last phase of *The Waiting Journey,* paying it forward.

By now, you've faced struggle, embraced the pause, trusted timing, fought for focus, leaned into faith, practiced prayer, guarded your heart, learned fasting, waged warfare, chosen praise, faced setbacks, and discovered gratitude as a weapon.

The final step is to let what you've learned overflow. Waiting isn't just about what you receive; it's about who you become and how your growth blesses others.

# CHAPTER THIRTEEN NOTES

**Reflection Pause:** Think about your own season of waiting. Who could you encourage, serve, or surprise with a gesture of generosity right now?

# EPILOGUE
# The Gifts I Didn't Expect

## Looking Back on the Wait

When I look back on those years of waiting, it's not just the pain that stands out. I remember the tears, the kind that soaked my pillow in the dark, and the quiet nights when I wondered if God had misplaced my name. The silence could feel suffocating, pressing in until I thought I'd break. But with time and distance, something else comes into focus: the strength that slowly took root in me, the lessons I couldn't have learned any other way, and the unexpected gifts that showed up in places I never would have chosen.

Back then, the wait felt like it was draining me dry. Every delay seemed like a thief, stealing time, joy, and dreams I'd counted on. I pleaded for shortcuts, for anything that would hurry the ending along. But now, looking back, I see it differently. The waiting didn't defeat me; it refined me.

## The Gifts Along the Way

The wait carved out endurance I didn't know I had. It built compassion for others in their own waiting. It taught me to appreciate the small things, to laugh in ridiculous moments, and to have faith that went deeper than my feelings.

Those weren't gifts I asked for. Honestly, if I'd had the choice, I wouldn't have picked them. I wanted answers, not patience; open doors, not lessons in character. But the gifts I received are the very ones I now treasure most.

- **Endurance**—because I learned I can survive what once felt impossible.
- **Compassion**—because pain expanded my capacity to sit with others in theirs.
- **Perspective**—because time showed me that not everything I thought I needed was essential.
- **Laughter**—because sometimes you have to laugh or you'll collapse.
- **Faith**—because I discovered God isn't only faithful in the finish line moments but also in the messy middle.

Those are the gifts I didn't expect, and they've outlasted the pain that once consumed me.

## What Waiting Revealed

Waiting also exposed the cracks. It revealed the fears I had tried to bury, the doubts I had tried to hide, and the ways I had tried to control what wasn't mine to control. Waiting pulled those things to the surface, and as painful as it was, I needed to see them.

But waiting also revealed something bigger: God's steady hand. His presence when I thought I was alone. His timing, which always felt late to me, ended up perfect. I once saw waiting as punishment. Now I see it as preparation.

That shift changes everything. When you stop seeing waiting as wasted time and start seeing it as sacred ground, your story flips. The very thing you cursed becomes the soil of your growth.

## Turning Outward

The biggest surprise was realizing my wait wasn't about me. It was meant to overflow. The strength I built wasn't for me alone. The compassion I carry now is meant to comfort others. The lessons I learned are intended to guide others.

I've come to see that waiting equips you to give. What once felt like a burden becomes a toolkit. The scars become maps for someone else trying to find their way. My waiting was never just for me; it was also for the people I'd meet later, the ones who needed to hear, *"I've been there too."*

## A Picture I Carry

One image will always stay with me: the palm trees outside my Florida home. During hurricanes, the wind bent them nearly to the ground. Rain beat against them, but their roots held. And when the storm passed, they straightened again, scarred, but standing.

That's what waiting did to me. It bent me low, sometimes so low I thought I would break. But I didn't. The roots God grew in me held steady. Like those palm trees, I rose again. Different, yes. Scarred, yes. But stronger than I ever imagined.

Now, when I see storms in someone else's life, I can say with confidence: you may bend, but you won't break. Roots hold.

## Celebration and Commissioning

So here's the truth: the waiting didn't end the way I imagined, but it ended with gifts I didn't expect. Those gifts are what I carry forward. They're what I celebrate. Not perfection, not polish, just the raw reality of a God who was faithful through the wait.

But this isn't just my celebration. It's also a commissioning for you. Because if you've made it here, to the end of this journey, you've been carrying your own weight. And just like mine, your wait isn't wasted. One day, you'll look back and see the gifts it gave you. And those gifts won't be just for you either; they'll be for the world you're called to impact.

So, take your endurance, your compassion, your laughter, your perspective, your faith, and pass them forward. Let your scars be stories. Let your lessons be lifelines. Let your waiting become someone else's hope.

## Closing

The waiting threatened to break me, but it gave me treasures I never expected. The greatest gift of all is knowing the wait was never wasted; it was shaping me to give.

Struggle shows weakness. Pause reveals protection. Timing builds trust. Focus steadies your eyes. Growth shapes your heart. Prayer connects you. Guarding protects you. Warring trains you. Fasting sharpens you. Praise shifts your posture. Setbacks and mistakes teach you grace. Thanksgiving grounds you. Paying it forward multiplies what you've gained.

And the epilogue? The epilogue celebrates the gifts you didn't expect, the treasures waiting to be left in your hands. Which is why the book closes with a Final Encouragement, written not as an ending, but as a letter sending you forward.

# Final Encouragement

Friend,

If you've made it this far, thank you. Thank you for walking through these pages with me, for opening your heart, for letting my story brush up against yours. That's no small thing. Sharing my journey has been personal, raw, and sometimes heavy, and the fact that you've carried it with me means more than I can say.

I don't know the details of your wait, but I know the weight of it. Maybe you're waiting for a child, a relationship, a healing, a breakthrough, or a dream that feels like it's slipping away. Maybe it's something you can name out loud, or maybe it's something hidden so deep no one else knows you're carrying it. Whatever it is, I need you to hear me clearly: you are not alone.

Waiting can make you feel isolated, like everyone else is moving ahead while you're stuck at a standstill. I know that ache. I know what it's like to scroll through photos of someone else's answered prayer while wondering why yours hasn't come. I know what it's like to cry until you can't anymore, then wake up the next day and do it all again. I know the hollow silence of unanswered prayers.

But here's what I also know: the wait is not wasted.

I didn't believe that in the middle of it. In the thick of my own waiting, I would have rolled my eyes if someone told me that. I didn't want lessons; I wanted answers. I didn't want growth; I wanted relief. However, looking back now, I can see the truth. Waiting wasn't a punishment. It was preparation. It was shaping me in ways I couldn't see at the time.

And I believe the same is true for you.

I know it feels long. I know it feels unfair. I know there are nights when you wonder if anything is happening at all. I've been there. I've asked the tough questions: Why me? Why so long? Why this way? I've begged God for shortcuts. I've tried to force my own solutions. And I've collapsed under the disappointment when none of it worked.

But I've also lived long enough to see waiting turn into more than pain. It turned into preparation. It grew endurance I didn't know I had. It softened my heart with compassion for others in their waits. It stretched my faith beyond feelings. It taught me to appreciate the trivial things. It carved out laughter even in hard places.

Those are the gifts I didn't expect. And they've outlasted the answers I thought I needed most.

If you're in a season where gratitude feels backwards, where praise feels forced, where prayer feels heavy, where setbacks and mistakes feel like they've ruined everything, hold on. Don't quit now. Don't believe the lie that this is wasted time. Something is being built in you.

I won't sugarcoat it. Waiting hurts. It bends you low. It strips away your sense of control. It tests everything you thought you believed. But you will not break. You're stronger than you think. And the roots God is growing in you right now will hold you steady when storms rage.

One day, you'll look back and realize that the very season you thought would destroy you was the season that shaped you most. You'll see how the delays taught you discipline. How did the disappointments deepen your faith. How the silence sharpened your ears to listen differently. How the longing gave you compassion for people you might have overlooked otherwise.

And you'll see that your wait wasn't just for you.

Because here's the secret: waiting equips you to give. The lessons you're learning now will become lifelines for someone else later. The scars you carry will become maps for someone else who feels lost. The patience, faith, and resilience you're building will spill over into your family, friendships, work, and community. The wait you hate now may become the very thing that gives someone else hope.

That doesn't make it easy. It doesn't erase the ache. But it gives meaning to the struggle. And sometimes, meaning is what gets you through another day.

So, take one more step. Whisper one more prayer. Wipe one more tear. Lift your eyes, even if only for a moment.

If all you can do today is breathe, then breathe and call that victory. If all you can do is whisper, *"I'm still here,"* then whisper it with all the strength you've got. That's enough. Don't measure your worth by how strong you feel. Sometimes the bravest thing you can do in waiting is simply not to quit.

And please know this: I'm cheering for you. I may not know your name or your story in detail, but I know the God who is writing it. And I know He doesn't waste waits.

With all my heart, I believe this: you will come through stronger, softer, and carrying gifts you didn't expect. Waiting is not the end of your story. It's the soil where new life is being planted.

Keep going, Friend. Not because it's easy, but because the wait is doing more than you can see.

Standing with you in the Wait,
**Carla**

# Appendix – Tools for the Waiting Journey

## 1. Practical Prayer Guide for the Wait

When words run out, here are short prayers you can whisper, write, or repeat.

### Honest Prayers

- "God, I don't understand."
- "God, I'm tired."
- "God, please don't leave me."

### Breath Prayers

- "Help me, Lord."
- "Thank You, Lord."
- "Be with me."

### Praise as Prayer

- "You are still good."
- "I trust You even here."
- "I will praise You while I wait."

## 2. Grounding Tools

Simple practices to steady yourself in the wait.

- Read and repeat a verse each morning.
- Keep a gratitude list.

- Place sticky-note reminders where you'll see them (mirror, car, desk).
- Use worship music to shift your atmosphere when emotions run high.

## 3. Pause Practices

Ways to lean into the pause as preparation.

- Journal what you're learning.
- Ask: *"What could this season be teaching me?"*
- Choose one small daily discipline (exercise, prayer walk, fasting from social media).

## 4. Focus Reminders

How to fix your eyes when distraction comes.

- Start your day with Scripture before screens.
- Limit comparison triggers (take a social media break).
- Ask a trusted friend to remind you of the truth when you start spiraling.

## 5. Growth Checkpoints

Questions to see how waiting is shaping you.

- What fruit of the Spirit (Galatians 5) do I see developing in me?
- What unexpected gifts have I noticed in this season?
- Where has my endurance or gratitude been stretched?

## 6. Guarding Practices

Protecting what God has grown in you.

- Identify triggers that weaken your faith (people, habits, environments).
- Speak Scripture aloud when lies or doubts creep in.
- Set healthy boundaries around your time, energy, and emotions.

## 7. Warring in the Wait

Tools for spiritual battle.

- Pray Scripture as declarations (Ephesians 6, Psalm 91).
- Fast from distractions that weaken you.
- Write out specific lies you've believed and counter them with truth.
- Gather prayer partners who can stand with you in the fight.

## 8. Fasting Helps

Practical ways to fast in waiting.

- Food fast (full or partial—consult your doctor first).
- Digital/social media fast.
- Entertainment fast (TV, games, etc.).
- Use fasted time for prayer, Scripture, journaling, or serving others.

## 9. Praise & Worship Prompts

When waiting feels heavy, use praise to lift your focus.

- Make a waiting playlist of songs that remind you of God's faithfulness.
- Sing even when you don't feel like it—let the music carry you.
- Write down 5 things you can thank God for today, no matter how small.

# Closing Blessing

Father, thank You for meeting me in every waiting place, through silence, struggle, prayer, and praise. Let patience become strength, gratitude become a weapon, and peace become my posture. May these reflections keep my heart anchored in hope and my spirit open to growth. Let every lesson take root and every seed of faith bear fruit.

Remind me that waiting was never wasted, that what You began, You will finish. Now, may I go in courage, walk in wisdom, and move with grace, until every waiting place reminds me there is purpose.

Made in the USA
Coppell, TX
11 February 2026

71735997R20085